MINI ENCYCLOPEDIA OF
GARDEN
PONDS

MINI ENCYCLOPEDIA OF
GARDEN PONDS

How to plan, construct and
maintain a vibrant pond that
will enhance your garden

LINDA ADKINS

FIREFLY BOOKS

A FIREFLY BOOK

Published by Firefly Books Ltd. 2012

First printing

Publisher Cataloging-in-Publication Data (U.S.)

Adkins, Linda.
    Mini encyclopedia of garden ponds: how to plan, construct and maintain a vibrant pond that will enhance your garden / Linda Adkins.
[208] p. : col. photos. ; cm.
Includes index.
Summary: How to plan, construct and maintain garden ponds, detailing various accompanying plants, animals and fish.
ISBN-13: 978-1-77085-009-5 (pbk.)
1. Water gardens. 2. Aquatic plants. 3. Freshwater animals. I. Title.
635.9674 dc23   SB423.A3556   2012

Library and Archives Canada Cataloguing in Publication

Adkins, Linda
    Mini encyclopedia of garden ponds : how to plan, construct and maintain a vibrant pond that will enhance your garden / Linda Adkins.
Includes index.
ISBN 978-1-77085-009-5
    1. Water gardens. 2. Ponds. I. Title.
SB423.A35 2012   635.9'674   C2011-907740-X

Published in the United States by
Firefly Books (U.S.) Inc.
P.O. Box 1338,
Ellicott Station
Buffalo, New York 14205

Published in Canada by
Firefly Books Ltd.
66 Leek Crescent
Richmond Hill,
Ontario L4B 1H1

Printed in China

Originally published by Interpet Publishing Vincent Lane, Dorking, Surrey RH4 3YX England
For Interpet:
Editor: Hilary Russell; Designer: Sue Casebourne; Photography: Linda Adkins, Myles Water, Rupert Parkinson, Sue Rose, Mary Webb; Production Management: Colin Gower Enterprises Ltd.

The aim of this book:

This book sets out to help you make the most of your pond and avoid some of the pitfalls so that your efforts result in a successful and vibrant pond. Something that is increasingly becoming a "must have" for any garden.

The information and recommendations in this book are given without any guarantees on behalf of the author and publisher, who disclaim any liability with the use of this material.

Contents

Introduction

When someone thinks "a pond would fit nicely in here" they are unwittingly taking the first step into one of the most compelling, diverse and rewarding interests they can develop and pursue in their own garden.

It can be hard work installing a pond but the benefits it will bring to any garden make the effort worthwhile. The aim of this book is to help you make the most of your pond and avoid some of the pitfalls so that your efforts result in a successful and vibrant pond—something that is increasingly becoming a "must have" for any garden.

Before rushing out to dig holes, buy equipment or commit to anything it would be well worth the time to consider what type of pond would be most suitable for you, your garden and your lifestyle.

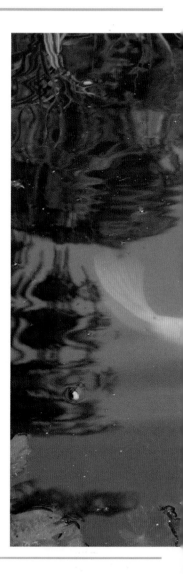

Opposite: The calm of a successful pond, both beautiful and compelling.

What style of pond?

Wildlife ponds

I doubt there could be an easier way of attracting a variety of native wildlife to a garden than by installing a pond and planting it appropriately. In size, a native pond can range from a plastic bowl sunk in the ground under shrubs to provide a base for amphibians, to huge constructions with rocks, pools at different levels, waterfalls, streams and reed beds. Wildlife-friendly ponds need not be uninspired and modest to be successful and attract a wide spectrum of native creatures that will enhance your garden.

The first creature that one associates with ponds are frogs. Not only the amphibians with the highest profile, they are also the most eco friendly way of controlling small garden pests like slugs, snails, grubs and insects. Less visible but equally effective are newts and toads —seldom seen, but voracious hunters. They don't need to have a pond to live in but are far more likely to stay in residence when there is a pond for them to visit and breed in.

Keep in mind though, that the settling of these native amphibians at your pond will be undermined if there is something living in the pond that will eat their spawn. Even in a well-planted pond, fish will decimate the naturally

Above: The frog depends on garden ponds to breed.

Above: This pond will attract wildlife.

Above: A pond will invariably attract damselflies to your garden.

occurring wildlife. It is a clear choice, either it is a wildlife pond, with no large fish, or not.

More fragile but possibly more attractive are some of the insects a pond will attract, like dragonflies and damselflies, not to mention the multitude of small winged insects a pond supports that will in turn support larger creatures, from garden birds to bats.

Your pond will form the foundation for attracting many creatures. Apart from the above examples, depending on its geographical location, a vibrant pond will attract creatures from garter snakes to kingfishers and from ducks to herons. In suburban areas, foxes will visit, while nearer the countryside, deer, rabbits and badgers are likely to put in an appearance.

Ponds and gardens are rapidly becoming one of the most important habitats for a huge variety of wildlife. Installing a wildlife pond will not only benefit native species and aid conservation, it will provide a restful and calming feature that people of all age can investigate or just plain enjoy as a feature.

Above: A modest fishpond can provide constant interest.

Small fish ponds

A modest fish pond under 222 gallons (1,000L), can still achieve many of the aims of a wildlife pond, although to a lesser extent. Even a tiny pond, carefully planted, can enhance a garden. If you are going to keep fish then make sure the pond is at least 3 feet (91.5cm) below ground and/or in a sheltered place to try and prevent the likelihood of it freezing over during the winter.

In the wild, each fish will have at least 35 cubic feet (1m³) of water to itself but in a pond most people would like to see at least a couple of fish. In order to support more fish with less space than in the wild, a fish pond

Above: This brick built pond fits neatly in a tiny garden.

Above: Small plants will quickly spread when planted in your pond.

Right: A mature, small pond with casual planting, a low maintenance addition for a small garden.

Above: A fish pond will benefit from some form of water movement.

will benefit from some form of water circulation. On the most simple level, a small pump to move the water will help keep a pond fresh, but unless the water is filtered the pond will become stale, especially if there are too many fish for the pond to support. Using a pump to aerate the water, by fitting a fountain or an external feature—such as a spitter or a waterfall—will further enhance the pond ecology and provide the sound of running water that can be so soothing. As long as provision has been made during construction to accommodate the necessary pipe work it is not difficult to add a filter at a later date to enable higher stocking levels.

Plants for a fish pond are most often chosen for their visual impact although most will also contribute to the ecology and biological balance. It depends on the position and the type of garden as to which plants are most appropriate but fairly natural planting will help to maintain the pond as a draw for wildlife.

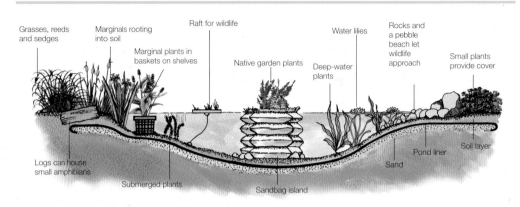

Grasses, reeds and sedges

Marginals rooting into soil

Raft for wildlife

Marginal plants in baskets on shelves

Native garden plants

Deep-water plants

Water lilies

Rocks and a pebble beach let wildlife approach

Small plants provide cover

Soil layer

Pond liner

Sand

Logs can house small amphibians

Submerged plants

Sandbag island

Above: A medium pond can accommodate an integral feature, a planted island for instance.

Medium ponds

A pond over 222 gallons (1,000L), being a large enough body of water and more able to maintain its temperature day to night and across the seasons, will therefore be able to support a wider variety of plants and fish. The increased capacity will also make it practical to fit a larger pump, a filter and a feature—if required.

Generally a pond this size will be stocked with larger fish that will grow even larger—and although much native wildlife will not be encouraged to live in and around such a pond it will still attract some. Mature frogs will often take up residence, garter snakes in particular will often favor such a pond and it is bound to attract herons.

The size and volume of water in a medium pond makes all manner of features possible that would be disproportionate to a smaller pond. A fountain is perhaps the most easily achieved, a waterfall is relatively easy to fit—especially using the preformed waterfall pieces that are widely available from aquatic and garden centers. Even a flowerpot can be attached to a pipe from the pump and angled to tip water back into the pond at nominal expense. Embellishing your pond to echo the style of your garden can be very rewarding.

Fish in a pond this size should be chosen carefully to ensure none will grow beyond the capacity of the pond—although it can be very effective to have one large fish. Your local aquatic center should be able to advise you on suitable fish and their care but having some types in mind before you start stocking would be a sound idea.

Large ponds

Few gardens have the space, or their owner the ambition, for a pond over 2,000 gallons (9,000L) but we can all dream. With a pond this big the options are much increased; not only would it be possible, but it would be practical to have enough planting to provide a more balanced habitat than in a smaller pond, and the potential for landscaping and features is also much larger. The bigger plants could be used to great advantage in such a pond, such as the architectural sedges that one thinks of as

Above: Few garden owners have the space for a large formal pond like this tranquil expanse of water.

Above: Shallow areas attract wildlife to the pond.

Above: An attractive decking island.

bulrushes, and the space for a vibrant lily means a large pond can be striking. Although allowing for a shallow area or beach will encourage some wildlife, the pond will support large fish and it is likely that you will succumb to temptation and go for specimen fish rather than wildlife.

You could really go for it, and construct a deck over the water, or even a small island, but unless it has occurred naturally a large pond is going to involve considerable expense.

Feature ponds

A less "natural" looking pond will still attract some wildlife but since it is the look of it that is paramount, a feature pond is usually defined by its surroundings. A pond in a formal paved area can be very effective, adding another element to an otherwise bare space. A slightly raised pond with a wooden deck surround is a popular feature—although one should ensure any moving water will not splash out. A defined shape whether a circle, a square or a quadrant (for instance) will sit well in a formally laid-out area of the garden.

The actual shape need not detract from its function as a pond but if considering a formal pond it is imperative to consider placement and access for filtration in the planning. It is a bit too late to wonder where to put a filter after the expensive slate paving has been finished! Historically popular are lily ponds, which often featured a statue in the center and were kept more for the lilies than fish – and why not? Many pond plants are strikingly attractive and can be as decorative a feature as a pond dedicated to fish.

Planning your pond

Safety in and around ponds

Worth considering before committing to any pond is safety.

Obviously any body of water can be dangerous, particularly to the very young or infirm. A pond does not have to be deep to be a potential hazard, so consider who will have access.

Very young children that are still unsteady on their feet may inadvertently stray into a pond but unless you are expecting hoards of kamikaze toddlers to invade your garden then a few simple precautions should prove effective.

There are a number of resilient grids that one can place over or in the pond to prevent people falling in but they do make maintenance and access difficult and are they really a good idea? Allowing children to think that ponds are safe is not wise—they are not. In practice we have found that the best way to keep very young children safe around ponds is to make them very aware of them. Spend time introducing them to the pond, engage their interest in the fish and any wildlife (while casually making sure they are aware the water is too cold to be pleasant), and the majority of small children will treat a pond with respect. Even if you are still unsure about their safety around a pond, you don't need to remove the pond. Not even the most vulnerable toddler will stay that way forever and in the long term, you are depriving yourself and the child of a valuable resource.

Make the pond less accessible by fencing it off temporarily. A play yard gate should be enough to protect a small pond, and a small picket type fence and gate will shield a larger pond. Keep in mind that even if you are unaware of it, your pond may have many other visitors, from frogs to foxes. Leaving space for these animals to get in and out of the area safely would be wise.

Often overlooked in planning a pond is the surfacing immediately around it. Especially on decking, damp surfaces are frequently slippery

Above: Ensure fountain or feature spray falls within the pond to avoid making surfaces slippery.

Above: Fencing off a pond will make it safer when you have children in your garden.

so ensure that any fountain or feature spray is confined within the pond area. This is even more important over the winter. It is unpleasant to slip on ice anywhere, but around a pond a simple slip can turn into a nasty fall. Ensure the area surrounding the pond does not stay damp by sloping the surroundings slightly away from the pond.

Electricity and ponds

As even the smallest pond will benefit from a pump to keep the water circulating, provision should be made for an electrical supply nearby—but preferably 7 feet (2m) away from the pond. Although it is simple to run an extension cord out to the pond, that shouldn't even be considered as a temporary measure because water and electricity mix far too well to be treated lightly. As with all garden-use appliances, pond equipment should be fed from a ground fault interruptor (GFI) outlet. Most outdoor and garage outlets are GFI, but check to be sure.

Do not be tempted to just run the pump cable back to the nearest outlet, then pave over it. For one thing, the cable could be damaged if the

Ground Fault Interruptor outlet

Secure fencing around pond

Ground Fault Cicuit Interruptor panel

Air pump

Above: Wiring your pond safely.

paving shifts and secondly it will be close to impossible to remove or replace the pump. For safety and ease of use, use a cable rated for outdoor use, either armored or in a conduit (or pipe) to protect it from accidental damage, to a fused, ground fault circuit interruptor (GFCI) panel close to the pond. If using conduit leave a length of string/cord in with the cable so that other cables can be pulled through if required.

There are kits available from most aquatic and garden centers for installing outside power and it is well worth considering these. At the very least, using a GFCI panel by the pond will make maintenance easier and safer. Bear in mind that once you do have an electrical point in the garden, you may wish to use it for things other than a pond. When fitting a GFCI panel for the dedicated use of the pond leave at least one switch free for any later requirements —lighting springs to mind. Fitting a waterproof external outlet (the same type as domestic outlets, but waterproof) will make the best use of the laid cable. There are quite stringent laws requiring permanent wiring outside the house to be certified (by a qualified electrician or competent person) or for plans to be submitted and approved before installation, often re-enforced by subsequent inspections. These statutes are not intended to restrict individuals from using their garden as they wish but to make domestic outdoor areas safer.

Since pond equipment is predominantly low wattage it can be installed safely and to code by the homeowner, if recommended electrical

Above: When planning features which require electricity remember pond equipment should be fed from a GFI outlet.

fittings are used as advised. The key to avoid breaking code is to ensure that any feed to the pond is plugged into an GFI outlet, making it by definition non-permanent.

If your chosen pond equipment requires more substantial wiring, it would be prudent to take the advice and services of a qualified electrician. Failure to do so may cause legal problems if the installation causes electrical problems and may prove problematic when selling the house.

Siting

Having considered which type of pond you want the next step is to decide where to put it.

There are a few areas worth avoiding—directly under trees in permanent shade is not good—unless the pond is to be a small affair to support, rather than house, wildlife. Ponds will benefit from partial sun although the majority of plants prefer full sun, which is not ideal for the pond as a whole.

Also to be avoided are sites near established trees with invasive roots that can puncture a pond or that may drop leaves or needles that will taint the water. Maple, oak and pine are particularly likely to cause water quality problems.

Wildlife ponds especially will benefit from being located near "wild" areas of the garden to provide cover and a habitat for wildlife. The siting of fish ponds is less crucial, as they are more often positioned for their effect on the garden, but bear in mind what is likely to go on around them.

A front garden pond visible from a busy street is especially vulnerable, as there is a deep rooted instinct in some people to throw things into water. It may spoil the enjoyment of your pond if you have to continually fish out balls, food wrappers, shoes, fruit and other items.

When considering placing a pond in a front yard or near the house, bear in mind what may already be in the ground. Municipal services are invariably laid under roads, and they will generally come to your house under the front yard. The position of meters will usually give a clue as to where they are laid. If the position of the supply lines are not marked or known, proceed with caution when excavating, because damaging or severing either the gas, water or electricity lines, sewage pipes or buried cables (such as phone or TV) will prove expensive. If you are thinking of positioning a pond where there may be installed services buried, refrain from buying a preformed pond until the area has been excavated—there may not be enough depth to put a pond below ground. It has to be fairly obvious that putting a pond on top of services that could be damaged by soil movement and may require replacing, repairing or inspecting one day is not wise—it is quite expensive enough to have a service line repaired without the added expense and disruption of removing a pond.

Try not to position a ground level pond near a path or drive where bicycles, cars, or wandering dogs may be. Even if your dog is sensible and you can trust all your visitors, a slightly raised

Above: Spend some time considering where to site your pond. This situation is ideal for a wildlife pond.

Above: If your pond is to be near the house, bear in mind the services which may be in the ground already.

pond is prudent and will prevent run-off from the surface from flowing directly into the pond.

There is no reason why a pond cannot be inserted into a slope—which can be utilized to great effect as a back drop for the pond—but the slope above the pond should be stabilized to prevent run-off from tainting the water.

Feature ponds should be placed for effect, keeping the above points in mind. Make sure the main feature is as visible from around the garden as it deserves to be.

A pond will enhance the biology, appearance and use of your garden. Make any raised walls high and wide enough to sit on (where accessible) or provide a paved area for access or seating and the pond will become the focal point in your garden.

Above: Any raised walls high and wide enough to sit on will make the pond the focal point in your garden.

Making the pond

Construction

Deciding which type of pond and where to put it is the first step—deciding how best to achieve the desired pond is another matter. The construction is sometimes defined by the location chosen, but installing a pond can be a daunting prospect. The chances of finding an irregularly shaped pond that will fit exactly into a pre-determined space are slim but there are advantages to preformed ponds—especially for a first pond. With a defined shape, many of the decisions are already made, shape, capacity and planting shelves, all there in a neat package.

Preformed ponds

Take a look around aquatic centers and find out which shapes and sizes are available, but before you start, beware of a common pitfall. More often than not preformed ponds are displayed vertically, for practical reasons, and even a modest pond looks huge when standing upright. It is all too easy to pick out and buy a pond that seems perfect, until you get it home, lay it on the ground and all of a sudden, in situ, it looks very small.

Measure the space you want the pond to occupy before you go looking and take a tape measure along; it could save you from buying the wrong pond. Do not be afraid to lay ponds down and measure them and to stand back and try to get a feel for how it will look in your garden. If the staff object, then move on to another supplier because if this is to be your first pond, you will benefit from support and advice from an experienced and sympathetic retailer.

Preformed ponds come in an extraordinary variety of shapes and sizes. Generally they are made from thick plastic or fiberglass. Even though the plastic ones are moderately flexible, don't be fooled into thinking they will need more support and care to install than a more rigid fiberglass pond. Both types will need to be fitted carefully and fully supported or they will distort or even split.

Generally the more flexible preformed ponds are modestly sized, and start at about 65 gallons (300L). Although suitable for some wildlife they are seldom deep enough to prevent freezing over during a cold spell. This is worth considering when choosing what size pond you want. If a pond does ice over completely, the pressure builds under the ice, oxygen levels plummet and all but the hardiest of creatures, big and small will perish. However, positioning a small pond in a sheltered place, keeping a pump running in it over winter to circulate the water, or putting a cover over it on cold nights will help to keep even a tiny pond from freezing over in all but the coldest of spells. These smaller ponds are usually quite well designed with indents to lay pump cables in the edge, planting shelves and shallow areas or ramps for wildlife to access the pond.

Fiberglass ponds are also available in a variety of shapes and sizes but as with the smaller ponds, bear in mind that a modest pond will need to have one area at least 3 feet (91.5cm) below ground level to protect fish from severe weather. Less suitable to support wildlife, these ponds seldom have any provision for electrical supply or wildlife entry to the pond although most have planting shelves. When deciding, lay it on the ground and consider the planting shelves. You will not want plants obscuring your view of the pond, so either turn the pond around until the shelves are to the back or sides, or select a different design.

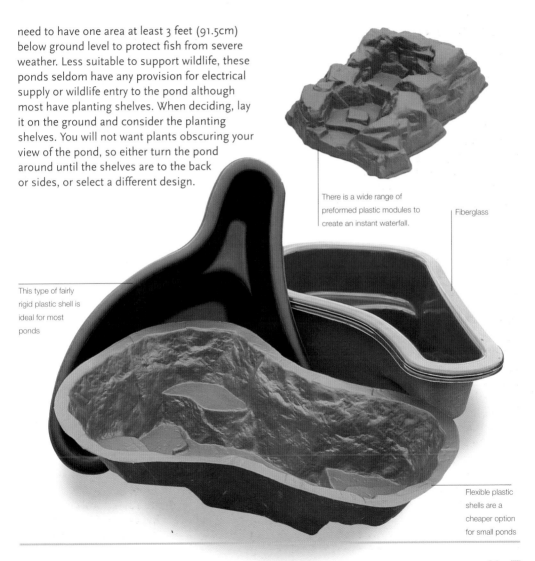

There is a wide range of preformed plastic modules to create an instant waterfall.

Fiberglass

This type of fairly rigid plastic shell is ideal for most ponds

Flexible plastic shells are a cheaper option for small ponds

Installing a preformed pond

Position the pond where you are happy with it, then mark the ground around the edge so that you know where to start digging. Unless it is a symmetrical pond don't turn it over and draw around it... that's not going to work!

Before starting on the ground work, stand back. Check that it achieves the effect you are after, then walk away and view it from all angles, even from an upstairs window. It is far easier to move the drawn shape than to re-position the pond later.

If you are planning a raised wall, waterfall, stream or any other feature, build a mock-up with cardboard or loose bricks and take the time to consider the whole effect.

When you have a clear idea of the look and function of your pond and any attached features, you will doubtless also have in mind what sort of use you wish to achieve, be it a wildlife pond, a generic fish pond or a feature. To get the best from any of these types of ponds you may need to fit, or add at a later date, pump(s), filtration, water clarifiers and even lighting. These will all need certain provisions—hosing to connect them, accessible placing for maximum effect and ease of maintenance, electrical supply, even control systems. It is too late to install many of these discreetly once the pond is fitted. Even if you have no immediate plans to invest in sophisticated additions, it would be well worth researching available equipment and making provisions for it in your plans.

It is essential to keep a spirit level and a plank on hand to lay across the hole to check that it is level. Water will always be level but if the pond is not there will be areas of pond liner visible and capacity unused. If the location you have chosen is not level, and cannot be easily made level so that rainwater will run away from the pond, rather than into it, it would be wise to raise the

Fiberglass

An excellent material for pond shells.

Firm plastic

Fine for a wide variety of projects. Strong, long-lasting and deep enough for fish.

Flexible plastic

Shells made from this more flexible plastic are usually only available in smaller sizes.

Above: If you are planning a raised wall, waterfall, stream or any other feature, build a mock-up with cardboard or loose bricks and take the time to consider the whole effect. It will be too late to make large changes once it's finished.

Above: A sloping garden isn't necessarily a problem. Make use of contours to enhance the area around your pond.

Left: A stunning waterfall feature.

pond slightly, even on the higher level to keep it above run-off.

Before you start to dig, check the stability of the ground that will form the outer edge of the hole. If it is loose or liable to crumble it is going to be nearly impossible to dig a defined hole —the edges will inevitably fall in as you dig and

will compact afterwards, potentially leaving the top edge unsupported. It may be necessary to put in a firm "collar" around the outside edge to support it. Depending on the soil texture and the scale of the pond this collar can be anything from a ring of firmly compacted earth to a row of loosely laid bricks/slabs to a trough dug in the earth and filled with gravel and concrete. All of which need to be level. If there are going to be walls or if the ground is sandy and likely to settle, dig suitable footings rather than a shallow collar around the top of the pond.

Before starting to dig, consider that topsoil is most often of a very different composition than the subsoil, and mixing it renders it all less than useful. Make two separate piles, one of soil, one of subsoil.

Cutting some posts or lengths of cardboard tube to the same depth as the planting shelves and base of the pond will enable you to easily measure down from your plank to check the depth of the hole. Then start to dig. It will soon be apparent if there are a large number of stones in the soil. Even the water in a small pond will be heavy, and a filled pond puts a lot of pressure on the sides and base. If there are stones close to the pond, they can puncture it, so remove all you can.

Line the hole with sharp sand and place the liner in when you think the hole is the right size and shape. Push and wriggle it around gently, then lift out again, and you will be able to see from the scuffed sand where the liner has touched. Keep digging away and refitting the pond until it barely touches the sides of the hole all around. Pay special attention to the base and shelves of the pond, as they will collapse or split if unsupported. Although it is useful to use sand to define the hole, sand can settle, be moved by burrowing insects and worms and even be washed away by rain—leaving a void under the

Above: Most preformed pond edges are designed to be covered. Dig a trench around the pond to make a base for the paving. Make a concrete collar around the pond edge.

pond. Keep the sand layer to a minimum and line the hole with old synthetic carpet, pond felt or root barrier membrane. This will enable you to establish firm, resilient support for the pond. The top 12 inches (30cm) of the pond can be backfilled firmly with subsoil once the lower parts of the pond are snugly positioned.

The top edges will benefit from being supported on a single row of loosely laid or cemented bricks if you have not put in a laid collar to ensure a solid edge for the pond. Before you decide that it fits, check the levels from side to side and back to front with your spirit level on the plank. It will be far too late to adjust it once it is firmly seated and full of water.

Most preformed ponds are designed to have the outside edges covered. As plants cannot grow into the material of a pond, do not be tempted to sod over the edge, or else it will slip off, either when it rains or when someone steps on it. Safer and more effective is a rigid surround that can be safely walked on.

Unless the pond is a very regular shape it will not lend itself to a surrounding deck, aside from which, decking invariably gets slippery with rain and ice and can prove a real hazard near a pond. A surround of flagstone, paving bricks, paving slate or cut slabs will be most suitable, and they

Above: Grout the flagstones with mortar.

Above: Lay paving on a bed of mortar. Slope the paving away from the pond to prevent rainwater from running into it.

can be made to look unobtrusive with careful installation, even though they will look stark when freshly laid. Some materials can leach chemicals into the pond when it rains, so check the material you have chosen by putting a drop of vinegar on to it—if it fizzes, the material is unsuitable unless it is sealed.

It might seem to be inviting disaster, but fill the pond with water and leave it to stand for at least 12 hours before you start to bed in the surround, as even the most firmly seated pond is likely to sink appreciably when it is filled, due to the sheer weight of the water.

Inevitably some concrete and earth will fall into the pond while you are working around it, and that is not good for the water. This won't matter though, because this initial fill should be removed when the surround is dry, leaving the pond clean and ready for use.

Using the firm surround beneath the lip of the pond as a foundation, remove any loose soil around the edge to leave sufficient depth to seat the surround in firmly. Be careful to remember, before it is too late, to leave a gap in the surround wide and deep enough to accomodate a cable (for the pump and perhaps lights) and even if you have no plans to install a filter at present, it is wise to leave enough room in a discreet corner to the side or back, for a 1-inch (25mm) hose, just in case you decide to add a filter or feature later. Placing the surround on a bed of concrete and grouting between the stone (or bricks) is the logical and durable method. Either buy bags of concrete mix or mix cement with three parts of sharp sand, but be sure during mixing to add a binder to prevent the chemicals in the cement from leaching into the pond. There are a number of products you can mix with concrete to seal it, the most easily sourced being polyvinyl acetate (PVA). Even with a good proportion of PVA in the mix, the exposed surfaces of the cement can still be crumbly. When all the work is finished and has cured, paint over the edges nearest the pond with either a pond-specific sealant or more PVA.

When the surround is set, empty the pond, removing any detritus that has dropped in from the cementing.

Consider the position of the pond with regard to the planting shelves, because unless it is in a sheltered area, tall plants can be blown off the shelves and into the pond (even medium-sized fish can inadvertently push pots off smooth shelves). Not only is this annoying, but it results in stones and soil littering the bottom of the pond, aside from damaging a tall plant. While the pond is clean and empty, select some smooth pebbles or paddle stones and affix them

to the leading edge of vulnerable shelves with a credible adhesive. Double sided butyl tape or pond mastic should do the trick. Check the grouting around the edges of the pond. It may have shrunk back from the pond as it dried, and infilling between the pond and the underside of the grouting with mastic will stop water from seeping through the gap and washing away the infill.

Advantages of preformed ponds:
◆ The shape is clearly defined.
◆ Planting shelves are invariably included.
◆ They are more durable in many ways than a flexible liner that can be torn or punctured.
◆ They can be removed and positioned in another location.
◆ Unlikely to be pierced by invasive roots from trees or shrubs.

Disadvantages:
◆ You are limited to their size and shape
◆ Planting shelves are usually flat, plants can easily be knocked off by boisterous fish or strong wind.
◆ They are awkward and unwieldy to position.
◆ They are seldom deep enough to ensure protection against extremes of weather.
◆ For a similar outlay one could buy and install a liner pond with a pump, filter or waterfall.

DIGGING THE HOLE FOR A LINED POOL

1 Mark out the shape with a garden hose. Dig the shelves deep enough for a plant basket.

2 Dig the deeper central area of the pond.

3 Use a mattock to level the base and remove any stones or sharp objects which might puncture the liner.

4 Ensure that the marginal shelves and the edges are level in all directions using a spirit level.

Lined ponds

Note that lined ponds are appropriate only in regions where temperatures never dip below −15°F (−26°C), Their best feature is that you dig exactly the pond you want, and then buy the liner to fit.

Excavating

Start your ground works as for a preformed pond, with one major difference—you will be working to your own defined outline.

Dig out the shape to a depth of 10 inches (25cm), avoiding completely vertical sides since they are very likely to collapse. Better to slope the sides inwards slightly. Choose where to put planting shelves, mark them out and continue digging.

As with installing a preformed pond it is important to remove any stones that may pierce the liner. Tempting though it may be to dig a concave crater shape, remember that if you plan to have a pump, with or without a fountain, or any deep water plants, it will be important to have a flat area at the bottom of the pond. It is worth laying a couple of paving slabs or concrete blocks in the bottom to get a flat base, especially if you decide to install a center piece.

When you are happy with the shape, size and depth, tidy it up, check for stones and adjust the level areas. Planting shelves will be far more useful if they slope back towards the wall of the pond, and adding a raised lip around the edge of the shelf will also help to keep plant pots in place. Almost last, stabilize the edges, as they may have been disturbed during the digging. Compact the earth firmly and lay stones, bricks, blocks or even a bed of concrete around the top edge to keep it tidy. Build any walls above ground, because unless they are to be filled behind with soil, single brick walls are unlikely to be effective. Building a double skin wall is best, giving strength and support and allowing a good width of wall to hold the top of the liner in. Finish off by evening up the contours with damp sharp sand and line the horizontal areas of the pond with pond underlay, pond felt or synthetic carpet.

Buying the liner

There are a number of different materials available for pond liners:

Polyvinyl chloride (PVC), a fairly rigid material, is entirely adequate for small, regular-shaped ponds and can be cheaper than other materials. It is, however, not stretchy and will need meticulous folding and creasing into place. It is also more vulnerable to tearing and damage from stones and piercing from invasive roots. Adding a root barrier membrane and/or pond felting will increase the cost but may be necessary. Make sure that any PVC sheeting you choose is intended for use as a pond liner and is UV-protected or it will rapidly become brittle.

is generally considered the best pond liner. Marketed under a variety of trade names it is essentially a similar material whatever the make, although it would be advisable to go for a known brand and a thickness of 1mm or above. If you do find a supply that is considerably cheaper then be wary, it may be of lesser quality or thickness. Both flexible and malleable, butyl is easier to fit to complicated shapes and more forgiving, being less inclined to tear. Even so, if evidence of strong roots was found when digging the pond it would be wise to use a root barrier membrane.

Defining how much liner is required is relatively straightforward but it is well worth taking the measurements with you when buying your liner and asking the retailer to check your figures—a liner will be entirely useless if it is not big enough.

Both PVC and butyl liners are available either as a length cut from a roll or in pre-cut packages, but inevitably, some will be measured in meters, some in feet, so be sure to take both measurements with you.

Measuring up for a liner

This is going to require some math:

Measure the pond at its longest length, width and depth, in feet for ease of use.

The liner needs to be the dimensions of the width times the breadth, with enough added to allow for the liner to go down one side and up the other, and an additional 6 inches (15cm) on either edge to allow for sufficient spare to lap over.

This allowance gives you a margin for trimming the liner to size.

First calculation: Double the depth and add twice the 6-inch overlap (1ft).

Add the answer to the length of the pond to give the length of the liner.

Add the same number to the width of the pond to give the width of the liner.

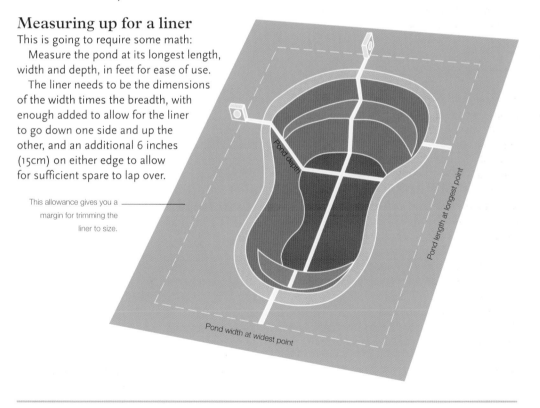

Pond depth

Pond length at longest point

Pond width at widest point

Example:
For a pond 13ft long, 9ft wide and 3ft deep.
First sum: double the depth and add 1ft. The
depth is 3ft, so 2 x 3ft = 6ft.
Add 1ft to give a 6in overlap on each side.
6ft + 1ft =7ft.
The liner length required will be the length of
the pond, (13ft) plus 7ft = 20ft.
The liner width required will be the width of the
pond (9ft) plus 7ft = 16ft.
The liner size required will be 20ft x 16ft.

If the liner you choose is sold by the meter
rather than the foot, convert the measurements
into metric. In this case 20ft = 6m, 16ft = 5m (to
the nearest meter). The liner required will be a
minimum of 6m x 5m.

If in doubt, provide your measurements to your
supplier and get them to calculate it for you!

If the pond is a defined and regular shape, a
flat-bottomed rectangle for instance, with flat or
no planting shelves, most manufacturers will
make up a box liner with welded and chemically
sealed seams to fit your pond exactly. Obviously
this is not a free service, so not only will the liner
work out to be more expensive but you will have
to measure very carefully to ensure a good fit.

Fitting a pond liner

Lay the cut liner over the pond and gently work
it into position, ensuring it is going to reach
over the edges in all directions. The next task is
to lay it carefully into the bottom of the pond
and arrange any folds and creases neatly.

Unless it is a small pond, or you have
extraordinarily long arms, getting into the pond
is the easiest way of getting it right, but take off
your shoes or replace them with soft soled
shoes first. Damaging the liner before it is even
fitted would be irritating to say the least.

When the liner is laid into the lower levels of
the pond, check there is still enough overlap all
around the top edges of the pond allowing for the
rest of the laying in, then begin to fill the pond
with water, laying in folds and shapes as it fills. If
the lay of the liner permits, deliberately create a
fold around the leading edge of the planting
shelves to further hold plants in place. When the
pond is full to within 6 inches (15cm) of the top,
lay the top edge over and lay in any folds neatly.
Allow the pond and liner to settle, preferably
overnight to minimize the risk of it pulling and
straining at a later date. Trim to shape, allowing
the maximum amount of liner that you can

Above: When you get your pond liner home check it
carefully for tears and imperfections.

FITTING THE LINING

1 Lay in a cushioning underlay if the ground is stony, and use a root barrier version if there are potentially invasive roots.

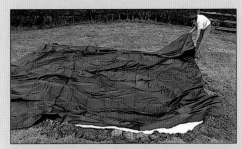

2 Spread the liner carefully over the hole allowing enough extra for it to fold into the hole.

3 Take off your boots or wipe off as much mud and stones as possible then lay the liner as flat as you can in the base and arrange the creases up the sides and shelves. A ridge along the front of the planting shelves would be useful.

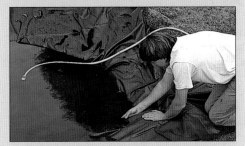

4 Fill the pond gradually, laying in the creases as the water pushes the liner into place.

manage to tuck in or dress over.

Finish off the edge as described earlier, with slabs, blocks, bricks or capping stones, all bedded with sealed concrete, not forgetting to leave access to the pond for cables and hoses as required. When all the surround has set and dried off, which can take days—empty the pond and remove any debris that fell in during the finishing.

Above: Disguise pond liner edges with stones.

Advantages of a pond liner:

◆ The shape and size can be tailored to your yard.

◆ Planting shelves can be installed in the correct places, and angled or lipped to keep plants in place.

◆ They are relatively easy to fit.

◆ The pond can be dug to a suitable depth.

◆ A pond can be installed in an area that has obstructions and digging problems by working around them.

◆ Although it varies with size of pond and type of liner, liner can be a fraction of the price of a preformed pond.

Disadvantages of a pond liner:

◆ Awkward shaped ponds can make it difficult to keep folds and creases discreet.

◆ Can be pierced and damaged by herons, large birds hunting for snails, rodents and other animals.

◆ Almost impossible to re-use in a different position.

Solid build/install ponds

Then of course there are the other methods for making ponds:

Concrete/constructed ponds

Although it may seem superficially easier to construct a pond in the manner of a building, using block or brick-build and slab work either above or below ground, pond construction involves elements of construction that do not occur in usual building practice.

The main consideration is the sheer weight of water. A five gallon bucket of water weighs just over 41lbs (18.5kg). A pond 10ft x 10ft and 3ft deep will contain 1,875 gallons of water which weighs in at an astounding 15,637lbs, nearly 8 tons, or for the metrically inclined, over 8,000kg.

By any measure that is heavy.

Any medium to large pond will require substantial foundations, at least 2 feet (61cm) below the base of the pond and very substantial sides, more so if they are above ground. Below ground the pressure of the water will load back onto the subsoil, which, unless it has been disturbed, should be well compacted. Above ground, supporting structures will be necessary.

If the ground the pond is built on remains stable, the pond will not shift or distort. Unfortunately, virtually all soil shrinks and contracts with temperature and varying moisture level so you cannot rely on it to support your pond. It must have an integrity of its own and be sufficiently strong and bonded into a single unit that will not distort.

You are going to need a structural engineer to define the construction for a medium to large pond.

Above: Formal shapes are usually easier to create with concrete or block work.

To illustrate: When building dry docks for use on a canal, engineers usually construct a "floating" dry dock which could, theoretically, be lifted out of its position and moved as single unit. For a dock 70ft long, 10ft wide and 6ft deep (a size to suit most canal boats), the reinforced concrete structure that sits below ground will be at least 10 feet (3m) thick.

That is, proportionally, the sort of construction required to attempt a waterproof, constructed pond. In practice, medium and large constructed ponds are almost inevitably going to settle, shift and crack enough to leak and it is more common practice when constructing a built pond to line it with a PVC-, preferably a butyl-, liner.

As with any other concrete in and around ponds, all building works close to, or in contact with the water must be sealed to prevent tainting the water. A common solution in constructed ponds is to line the build with a sealed render.

It is very important to consider the use of pond equipment and add-ons such as waterfalls, filtration, water clarification and so on before committing to any design. Check the "Planning your Pond" section as the same advice applies to constructed ponds.

Above: Below-ground construction is vital for ponds that have a defined, geometric shape, both large and small.

Above: Large, informal ponds are best suited to clay lining.

Clay ponds

If you are fortunate enough to have both the space and the budget for a pond over 20 feet (6m) both wide and long, then liner may not be the most practical method to use. As detailed in the previous section, large bodies of water are heavy enough to distort most methods of solid construction. They may also involve local water authority notification and approval. The authority may advise a flexible, malleable method of lining your pond, or lake! One other factor to consider, preferably in the planning stage, is your legal obligation to inform your local water authority if you are planning, filling or refilling a large pond. This does only apply to really large ponds but it would be worth checking whether there are any restrictions in place locally before progressing too far. It would be very frustrating to construct a large pond only to discover there were restrictions to filling it.

As with artificial ponds, lakes and canals built over the centuries that are still viable today, puddled clay is the most suitable material. Below ground and permanently wet, it will shift and adapt to any changes in the subsoil to maintain its integrity. The use and specification of clay is a specialized area, so it woud be best to seek out professional help, as the type and use of clay will vary depending on the type of soil on your property.

Although such a large pond is suitable for different treatment than smaller ponds, much of the same advice will apply, including provisions for filtration, lighting etc. These should be considered in the planning stage, not just after you've finished!

Renovating a neglected pond

It is often the case that one becomes the owner of a pond unintentionally, usually when moving into a house that already has one. Often, the last owner will have left some equipment and occasionally some instructions but all too often, it is just a pond, with no pump, filter or guidance.

Most ponds will tick along nicely for months with no care, but when you are ready to tackle it, roll your sleeves up and first: Define the pond, its size, construction and stocking.

Indulge in some detective work and search around the perimeter for pipes and cables – there may well be clues as to how it was maintained. There may even still be a viable pump buried in there somewhere.

If the water is stale and the plants seriously overgrown it might be worth buying or borrowing a holding tank or kiddie pool. Pump the top two-thirds of the water out into the pool and reclaim all that you wish to keep of the plants. They can be deposited in the pool to repot later. Any fish or wildlife should likewise be put into the holding pool.

Although you may not be inclined to keep the existing water, all the inhabitants of the pond, from plants to fish, will be used to their environment, and it will cause them less stress and potential damage if they are kept in the water they are used to.

Remove any failing plants, mucky water and debris from the pond. Top up with dechlorinated water, leaving enough space to replace the water in the holding pool. It may sound bizarre to replace the stale water, but if the pond was viable before, then the water must contain the ingredients for a good pond. If in doubt, take a sample of the water to be tested, but if you find

Above: This elderly wildlife pond had become stagnant. It has been cleaned out but is static now that most of the original water has been replaced.

healthy fish—or better yet, newts—which are very critical of water quality, then assume the pond is going to benefit from keeping much of its water.

Draining a pond down in this way will go a long way towards restoring it but usually, taking it gradually will prove less trouble.

Install a pump to get the water moving (large enough to power a filter if required later). If you do find a pump languishing in the water, your local aquatic center should be able to advise you

Above: Draining the pond down may be necessary.

about its use and whether any repairs/parts would be worthwhile. Take the pump in with you —describing it may not be enough!

Use a net to trawl out the debris from the bottom and take control of any plants, repotting and trimming them back to suit.

The more you investigate and get to know the pond the easier it will be to decide what, if anything, you need to do to keep it healthy. It is rather working backwards, but there is no reason to remove (fill in) a pond even if you hadn't intended to have one. A pond will always enhance a garden and doesn't need to be a lot of work if the basic guidance on stocking, feeding and maintenance is observed.

Why bother thinking about a pump or filter?

Usually, because you will find you want them.

The reason the earlier sections have mentioned filters, pipes and cables so often is because the massive majority of garden ponds do need filtration. In most instances it is not only a useful addition, it is essential to the success of the pond.

The primary reason is stocking levels, the number and size of fish any pond can support without filtration and water movement (although even a pond without fish will benefit from some form of water cycling).

In the wild, in ponds, streams, rivers and lakes, the fish population density will be far less than in a domestic pond. If considering how many fish there may be in a natural body of still water one would estimate less than 1 inch (25mm) of fish per square foot of water surface as the maximum. Any greater density than that and there would not be enough nutrients and oxygen to support the fish and inevitably, some would die until a comfortable stocking level was reached.

Moving water can support a slightly higher density. Swift-moving, well-planted waters slightly more.

Take a look into a river or lake sometime, guesstimate the water surface area, then see how many fish you can see? Even if there is a shoal of fish visible, it is probable that the ratio of fish to water surface is low.

Measure the area you have decided on for your pond and it may come as rather a surprise how few fish that area will support.

For example, a pond 6ft 6in x 3ft 3in, (2m x 1m), without a pump or a filter will support 21in (52cm) of fish. Sounds good? Not really, since even a small goldfish is 3 inches (7.5cm) long. So the pond will support seven fish, as long as they won't grow . . . which they will.

So better not to have seven fish, start with five? Five fish in a pond that size will not be very high impact—and that is the point.

We would all prefer to see the fish in our ponds, we might even aspire to have a couple of fish 10 inches (25cm) long. It's not going to work. That is why garden fish ponds need, at the very least a pump, and preferably a filter, so they can support enough fish to have an impact.

Additional features

Above: A fountain provides sound and movement.

There are many things you can add to your pond to make it higher impact, and not all need be expensive, although it is possible to spend a small fortune.

Fountains

As a starting point, adding a pump to a pond immediately makes it a more vibrant feature. Even if the pump is doing nothing more than agitating the water surface, it introduces movement, light and the sound of moving water, with the added bonus that it will freshen and oxygenate the pond. This is a low cost and maintenance effect that will not affect pond life although some plants will grow away from the splashing.

Slightly more sophisticated is to install a pump with a fountain.

Most pond pumps come with a range of fountain fittings, starting with a simple rosette that will give a moderately plain fountain. Beware of the height of a fountain, because if it is too high for the size of the pond, spray will splash out of the pond with the consequence of losing water and having a permanently damp (and possibly slippery) area around the pond. If the fountain seems too high, fit a fountain head with larger holes and the spray will be lower. Lilies will avoid splashing water, so if you plan for a lily, locate it away from the fountain.

Options may include a two or three tier fountain, a geyser (foaming spout) or a bell jet, where the water makes a dome around the riser.

Finer fittings can become blocked with pond debris, so it is likely to be necessary to fit a pre-filter on the pump, even something as basic as a piece of foam.

Not all fountains are attached directly to a pump, there are a number of fittings available that will produce a spinning fountain or twirling jets, most working on a similar principal to a lawn sprinkler with the water flow powering the rotation.

External spouting and pouring features

Even if a fountain in the pond is not to your taste, there are numerous options for introducing a feature that will return cycling water to the pond.

From plastic snails and concrete turtles with spouts in their mouths to elegant bronze ladies holding pouring urns, the range of spouting or pouring features is limited only by imagination.

At its most simple, a feature can be made from ordinary garden equipment; a hose from the pump into the base of a tipped flower pot, planter or watering can be entirely appropriate.

A contemporary garden might suit a stainless steel pouring feature, while a classic garden might look best with a lion spouting water. The variety is quite extraordinary, so rather than go out looking for a specific feature it is often more rewarding to visit aquatic centers, garden centers and DIY stores and keep looking until you find a

Above: An improvised pouring feature.

feature that will suit you and your pond.

Remember that any feature will be damp permanently. Avoid anything that will rust or corrode. Copper is the exception. As long as it is not a huge feature in a tiny pond, it will acquire a lovely patina with weathering but will cause only nominal changes to the water chemistry.

One key description to look for with any purchased feature is the phrase "frost-proof". Very few terracotta and china features will survive a frosty spell without cracking or flaking. Unless you are sure you will have the stoicism to put the feature under cover or wrap it up to protect it from frost every winter, stick to features that are guaranteed frost-proof. It might be worth mentioning here that even if the structure of a feature is frost-proof, the pump

and hoses are not. If they do freeze they are likely to be permanently damaged. Most ornamental features should be drained, the pump removed and be covered over the winter to prevent split hoses.

Pumps are not always included with a feature, so if you do not already have a pump with the capacity to feed your feature, take a photo and measurements with you to your local aquatic center and ask them which pump would be most suitable. It is important to check the size of any fitted pipe before selecting a pump, a narrow pipe will not allow for a heavy flow, a large pipe will require a greater capacity on the pump.

Right and below: Make sure your water feature is frost-proof if it is terracotta.

In-pond features

A centerpiece will suit many ponds. There are few of these marketed as dedicated centerpieces, but with a little imagination, statues and features that may be sold as free-standing features can be very effective in the center of a pond. A word of warning: if it is your intention to install a centerpiece statue or constructed fountain you will need to have a platform to support it without damaging the base of the pond. It is, of course, preferable to think of such a feature before lining the pond so that a solid base can be provided. If fitted to an existing pond, lay extra liner and underlay on the base of the pond before putting down sealed (paving) slabs to spread the weight of the feature. Either use round slabs or round off the corners of slabs to prevent them from piercing the liner.

A large feature will require a wide, integrated base, probably involving block work, but a smaller, shallower base can be constructed from (sealed) bricks or blocks.

Right: This lovely old millstone makes an attractive bubbling fountain.

Above: A preformed resin cascade, properly laid, is unlikely to lose water.

Waterfalls and cascades

Water cascades can be made out of almost any material: metal, plastic, resin, stone or concrete. Non-corrosive metals, such as stainless steel, can provide an attractive and contemporary feature in a modern garden. There are a limited number of such features available, one is more often than not looking at a custom feature, or a self-build.

It may sound tacky, but plastic should not be ruled out as the basis for a cascade although it rarely approaches a "natural" look. There are moulded, fairly inexpensive water courses and waterfall pieces available at retail. As a frost-proof, durable material, plastic can be a practical option, and particularly since it is reasonably easy to cut and shape it can be the material of choice to build your own cascade. To create a waterfall, pouring buckets, gutters, and pipes can be combined and used to great effect and at reasonable cost.

Moulded polystyrene waterfall pieces are durable and easy to fit, and almost indistinguishable from real stone. Resin cascades, many equally natural-looking, are available in a huge variety of shapes and colors, most designed to blend with, or complement particular types of stone. These are often very effective and dressed with matching stones and suitable planting can be very natural-looking.

Stone composite (and concrete) molded cascades are becoming less popular simply because they are very heavy, difficult to handle, inclined to crack and frankly, seldom as natural-

Above: Unless expense and time are of no object it is well worth considering pre-formed cascades.

looking as some of the resin pieces.

Built-in concrete and real stone cascades can look fabulous, but they do involve some pitfalls.

In order to be effective, a cascade needs to hold water and therein lies the first problem. Even building over a length of liner to prevent water loss can prove ineffective as water will flow under, around and through any block or stone work. Concrete (suitably sealed) may not

prove too extravagant but stone can work out expensive. As a rule of thumb, when you have decided (and budgeted) how much stone you will need, triple it. It takes a great deal of stone to entirely cover the lined course and make it look as if it sits naturally in position.

Although it is tempting to build or commission your own vision of a waterfall, unless expense and time are of no object, it would be well worth considering pre-formed cascades. Compared to the cost of real stone, they are reasonable. As long as they are laid sensibly they will not leak and perhaps best of all, if the pieces you select do not look quite right in your garden, you can change them.

Above: A steep, rock built waterfall.

Above: The step by step layering for constructing a stream. Dig, shape, line and dress.
Left: A delightfully rustic and natural looking stream.

Streams

It is not a long step from a running waterfall to a stream, either to feed a waterfall or as a feed in its own right. There is a slight logistical problem with streams though. They need to be sloping downward, if only slightly, to work. Therefore the pond (or sump) that the stream runs into—from where a pump feeds water back to the beginning of the stream—needs to be large enough to hold all the water that lies in the stream when it is flowing. It may seem obvious, but any stream needs to be in

Above: Streams need to be sloping downward, if only slightly, to work.

proportion to its pond or even a slight interruption in the flow will cause the pond to overflow.

If there is a reasonable grade (slope) where you wish to put a stream, overlapping preformed pieces would be a relatively simple way of establishing a short stream, but take care to mastic the overlap between pieces, especially on a shallow slope there is a distinct likelihood of water flowing back under the lip at connections. Even for a long stream, unless there is to be liner beneath to catch any stray water it is more practical to construct a stream in overlapping, or keyed in, sections to allow for the soil movement and expansion/contraction during temperature and weather changes.

Left: This bridge is both attractive and practical.
Below: Lapping preformed waterfall pieces in the course of a stream will provide interest.

Above: A raised reed filter bed, a pool or reservoir above the pond, sited so that water pours back into the pond.

Decorative filter beds

One feature that will add to the pond both esthetically and practically is a planted filter bed. Most often built in an adjacent pool joined to, linked to or flowing back into the pond. A natural filter bed is, in essence, a reservoir containing plants that will capture impurities and pollutants in the pond water, including fish waste, and use them for their growth—natural fertilizer if you will.

It will be necessary to pump water from the pond into the filter bed so that pond water flows through it, preferably slowly enough that it spends long enough in the filter bed to be rendered biologically clean.

The location and appearance of a filter bed is an entirely personal choice. A relatively shallow pool almost level with the pond and planted with low-level plants will have a similar impact to a flower bed, and can have some decorative bog or pond plants added to enhance the look.

The same, low-level pool could equally be planted with tall, architectural plants with a lower cover of filtering plants. Reeds and sedges are very effective filtering plants, but bear in mind that in their natural habitat these plants have to establish extensive and strong root systems to anchor themselves to banks and unstable soil. Their roots can pierce liners; using a root barrier membrane inside the pool would be prudent. Putting these large habit plants outside the area of the pond will make it feasible to have vigorous plants without them taking over the pond.

Even more striking is a raised filter bed, a pool or reservoir above the pond, located so that water pours back into the pond—either as a simple spout of water or over a cascade. Again, one can use low-level plants, but the choice here should be in proportion to the scale of the pond and the effect you wish to achieve. Some of the larger reeds and sedges can grow to more than 6 feet (1.8m) tall—and that is going to make quite an impact in an already raised pool.

Pergolas and canopies

Although they may not usually be an integral part of the pond, a frame over the top that provides shade and cover can be both decorative and useful. Timber-framed pergolas can look lovely and will serve a number of uses. Aside from providing a framework perfect for climbing plants, they shade the pond, keeping direct light off the pond and reducing algae levels, and disguise the pond from the air, making it far less obvious to herons.

Left: A timber pergola.

Pond protection

There are a number of pond predators that may affect your pond, causing disruption and taking your fish.

The heron is the most often blamed predator. Although it is a magnificent and rather improbable bird, a heron can decimate a pond. Although not out of spite, they will invariably take the favorite fish. The most visible fish is frequently the most appreciated, but by virtue of being obvious, it is the most likely to attract a heron's attention. They can often cause damage by stabbing at fish and accidentally piercing a liner, miscalculate their own size and attempt to take a fish far too large for them to even eat and frighten the fish enough that they may hide for weeks afterwards.

The most frequently used method for protecting fish from herons is fitting a pond cover net. This is only effective if the net is suspended at least 1 foot (30cm) above the water, otherwise a heron can stab through it. The disadvantages are that nets restrict access to the pond, will often get tangled in plants or contain them, and can spoil the appearance of your pond. Equally annoying, especially over a large pond, the net will sag and herons may use them to stand on and access the pond.

Anything that will make it difficult for a heron to approach the pond, like an outward sloping fence with wires, a thin cord at "tripping" height, an electric fence or something that appears to move—such as suspended CDs or floating, reflective pyramids—may deter them.

Left and above:
The most frequently used method for protecting fish from herons is a pond cover net.

One rather extravagant method of keeping herons out is to place a resilient metal or plastic cover over the pond.

In practice, most fish will have the sense to hide and avoid a heron but in an unprotected pond some fish losses are inevitable.

Few other predators are as well known—or get as bad press—as herons, but there are some. Kingfishers and racoons will take small fish. Garter snakes can—and do—take medium-sized fish, as will some cats and depending on your location, other mammals. Ultimately it is another choice to make, keep your pond open, accessible and vulnerable to "poaching" by wildlife, or rather, masked by protection.

Above: Fish attract hungry hunters.

Above: A large net is a useful investment and stops filters and pumps from becoming clogged with autumn leaves.

Above: A decorative heron by your water *may* discourage the real bird from poaching fish.

Just add water

It sounds simple, add water and a hole in the ground becomes a pond. However, the water is actually the most important part of a pond and it is well worth taking a little time to get the quality of it right—from the start.

Inevitably, however a pond is constructed, finishing its edge and "bedding" it into position while it is full of water is likely to result in it containing tainted water that will need removing when all the ground works around are stabilized. Once your hole in the ground is ready to be a pond there are a number of considerations to take.

One that has already been mentioned is that there may be restrictions on filling a large pond from the municipal water supply. In certain circumstances there may be a charge for the fill. Clearly, if the pond is smaller, there are no such restrictions—unless there are watering restrictions in force.

Unfortunately, as any aquarist already knows, tap water is treated to sterilize it, therefore making it unsuitable for pond life. The reasons why are due to our life style, and the requirements of aquatic life.

If a bucket of tap water is left outside in full sun it will rapidly develop algae and, depending on the temperature and environs, may contain insect larvae within a week, and possibly even water fleas.

This is totally natural, but we prefer our water to be "clean." None of us would be happy if our tap water contained mosquito larvae, bloodworm or green algae—baths just wouldn't be the same.

Your local water authority filters and cycles water before residential use. In the past they would infuse the water with chlorine gas which would burn off when the water was exposed to air, and was relatively unstable. The preferred treatment for maintaining "clean" water is chloramine which is added to municipal water to stop the growth of aquatic life.

Since we do have clean tap water these treatments work, but for that very reason the chemicals in tap water will not support the beneficial bacterial and micro-organisms that mature pond water requires and it can actively damage pond life. Obviously there are few sources of untreated water widely available to most people, but there are commercially available solutions. Dechlorinators convert chloramines into gas, which dissipates harmlessly, and the more sophisticated dechlorinators will also neutralize other heavy metals from the water and render it suitable to support aquatic life. As the main role of a dechlorinator is to release chloramines as gas, they should not be poured into the pond if it contains any aquatic life. The water should be treated and allowed to stand (to let gasses clear and the water achieve the ambient temperature) before adding to the pond.

As water condition is crucially important to a healthy pond, setting it up to maintain a good biological balance is key. Aside from problems caused by impurities in the water, an understanding of the natural processes will prevent many common pond problems.

The nitrogen cycle

In any freshwater environment, from a pond to a lake, river, bucket of water or fish tank, the nitrogen cycle is the same.

Aquatic creatures, from water fleas up to fish and amphibians including every creature in between, eat, process their food and excrete waste—some as solids in droppings but the majority in the form of ammonia, much of which is excreted through their "skin" or gills.

High levels of ammonia are poisonous, which is why an overstocked, or overfed and under-filtered pond will become toxic, smell bad and result in fatalities unless steps are taken to amend the imbalance. In fish tanks this is achieved by filtering the water vigorously and partially changing the water every one to two weeks. In a pond we would try to avoid water changes and establish a natural cycle, usually with the aid of a filter, to process this waste.

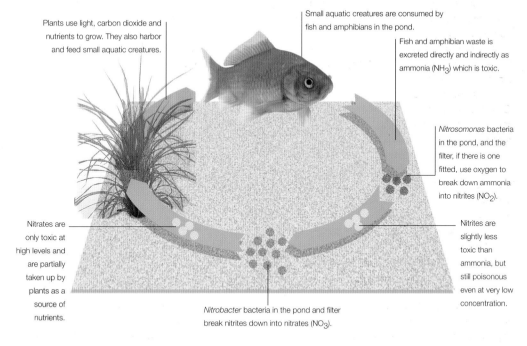

Plants use light, carbon dioxide and nutrients to grow. They also harbor and feed small aquatic creatures.

Small aquatic creatures are consumed by fish and amphibians in the pond.

Fish and amphibian waste is excreted directly and indirectly as ammonia (NH_3) which is toxic.

Nitrosomonas bacteria in the pond, and the filter, if there is one fitted, use oxygen to break down ammonia into nitrites (NO_2).

Nitrates are only toxic at high levels and are partially taken up by plants as a source of nutrients.

Nitrites are slightly less toxic than ammonia, but still poisonous even at very low concentration.

Nitrobacter bacteria in the pond and filter break nitrites down into nitrates (NO_3).

Above: The nitrogen cycle in the pond.

The primary waste, ammonia, is the starting point of the nitrogen cycle.

As soon as ammonia is present, bacteria will break it down into nitrite. These bacteria occur naturally but will take 10–14 days to occur in a new pond. If the water has not been dechlorinated the bacteria will be far slower to develop as will the other beneficial bacteria.

Paradoxically, nitrite is even more toxic to aquatic life than ammonia, and high levels will quickly prove fatal, not the least because—as with any water-borne pollutant—their presence excludes oxygen from the water. Fortunately, the bacteria to break nitrite down into nitrate, which is the main nutrient for plant growth, will arrive as the nitrite levels build. So, over the space of 30–60 days, the bacteria in the pond will break waste down into fertilizer, which grows plants, which are eaten and turned into waste again.

Good bacteria

In natural bodies of water, untainted by pollution, these "good" bacteria are present already, in the water, in the gravel, surrounding soil, etc. in sufficient quantities to break down any waste created in this natural cycle.

Due to higher than natural stocking levels, even in a well-established pond it is necessary to introduce a far greater underwater surface area where these good bacteria can thrive, and to have a system in place to remove excess debris, proteins and surplus nitrates.

A shallow silt layer in the base of an established pond is performing a useful function by maintaining these bacteria, but they need high oxygen levels to survive so are best maintained in moving water. Hence the importance of having moving water in some form, and the easiest way of introducing a huge, well-oxygenated surface area for bacteria to establish is to fit a filter.

The majority of filters perform a dual role. They will trap floating debris, giving mechanical filtration to keep the pond water looking clean. The media in a filter perform the invisible but possibly more important role of providing an environment for the good bacteria, therefore supplying biological filtration. These bacteria can be decimated quite easily by rinsing sponges in tap water, topping up the pond with more than 10% un-chlorinated tap water or using strong pond treatments.

Initial water quality

Before deliberately adding fish to a new pond, bear in mind that a newly-filled pond is nothing but sterile water, it is not pond water. There are many products on the market that will help to mature the pond water (and any filter), and most contain live bacteria to "seed" the pond (and filter). However good many of these products are, adding a bucketful of water from a healthy established pond (to de-chlorinated water) will go a long way to "seeding," but time is one of the most important factors in maturing.

There is a catch-22 situation with ponds. A pond will not have the full range of beneficial

Above: This new pond is going through an almost inevitable algae bloom as the water matures.

bacteria until it contains fish but it should not be stocked until the bacteria are established. Using a combination of dechlorinated water and biological starters will help, but just a quick mention—if the filter has an ultraviolet (UV) unit fitted, leave it turned off until the pond has been running for at least 10 days or the bacteria will not be able to colonize the filter.

Once the water has been prepared, mature the pond by running it as if it were already stocked. Keep the pump running, install any filters or features and establish plants, both for their contribution to the set-up biology and for the shelter they will give to the water.

After the system has been running for a minimum of seven days, have the water tested to find out how it is progressing.

Above: This well-established pond is ready for fish to be added.

WATER TESTING

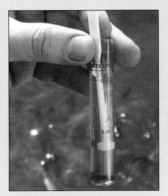

1 Aquarium test strips are ideal for early tests on a new pond at home.

2 The most crucial tests on a day-to-day basis are ammonia and nitrite.

3 Some raised levels are inevitable as the pond settles.

Water testing

Don't be intimidated by water testing, it is quite easy to understand and doesn't require a chemist's white lab coat. Most aquatic centers will be able to do a four-part test for you (for a nominal fee), which is useful, as their staff will usually interpret the results for you. Most tests require 1½ tablespoons (20ml), about an inch (25mm) in the bottom of a jam jar or water bottle will be enough.

The usual tests, and the three most useful to assess pond water quality, are ammonia, nitrite and nitrate. In a new pond that has had its biology kick-started, the initial test usually shows low ammonia, raised nitrite and low nitrate. Although very low or zero levels are preferred, some raised levels are inevitable as the water settles.

The fourth test most often offered is pH and it is very important that a new pond is tested for this. pH is the measure of acidity or alkalinity. Neutral is pH 7, over 7 is alkaline, under is towards acid. The pH of tap water varies from area to area depending on the local geography but as long as the pond tests between pH 6.5 and 8.5 it is acceptable to the majority of aquatic life, plants, fish and smaller creatures. With a newly-built pond there is always the risk that chemicals from stones, or run-off from soil or concrete will have tainted the water. If the pH is over 8.5 (alkaline) it is very likely these are the causes. Although it is possible to buy chemicals to adjust pH or buffer it, it is more sensible to solve the imbalance by doing a large or complete water change and sealing any exposed surfaces that may be contributing to the problem.

There are water-testing kits available and many people choose to do their own water tests at home. In most cases, testing is substantially unnecessary except for an annual check (or if there is an obvious problem). Although it is worth investing in a kit, it will become less accurate with age and may give misleading results, so keep an eye on the "use by" date on any tests and discard when it is out of date.

Although you may be eager to start stocking with fish, it is worth waiting until the water quality is good, any reputable aquatic center will decline to sell you fish unless the water seems ready—as they have a legal duty of care. It is traumatic enough for fish to be netted, bagged and moved to a new environment; they will be liable to all manner of unpleasant infections, parasites and maladies if the pond they are going to is not really ready.

Establish pond water quality

As any pond matures, pH differences can creep in that will be detrimental to the health of the pond and its occupants—it is well worth having a water test if any of the plants or fish are failing to thrive or there is an appreciable change in the color of the water.

Dark or peaty-looking water is usually becoming acidic. Normally caused by rotting leaves and vegetation in the pond, these may also cause an oily film on the water surface

which should be skimmed off, as it excludes oxygen. The easiest way to do this is to push a bowl or bucket into the water until the rim is just below the surface—the water tension and the oil film will run into the bucket to be discarded.

Even a healthy pond will, after a period of years, contain a deep enough layer of silt to be hosting anaerobic bacteria that will affect the water balance. Scooping this out one net-full at a time in the morning (to avoid the disturbance and leaving the pond short of oxygen) or taking the drastic step of cleaning the pond out will be necessary.

Oddly cloudy water may well test just fine for all the test parameters and the fish and plants will be perfectly happy, as long as the cloudiness is not suspended algae that will leave the pond short of oxygen overnight. Cloudiness due to suspended particles is only perceived as a problem by the pond owner!

It will be necessary from time to time to top up a pond, either because of a partial water change, loss from evaporation or leaks. It will not adversely affect the pond if tap water is added gradually as long as the volume is not over 10% of the pond volume at any one time. The addition of dechlorinated water is one factor—the other is temperature. Tap water is invariably considerably colder than pond water. Introducing large amounts will stress the fish—they are not well adapted to abrupt temperature changes. If a large top-up is necessary, fill a receptacle (bucket, kiddie pool etc.) with tap water, dechlorinate and leave to stand for 8–12 hours to achieve a more compatible temperature.

Rain water from a water barrel can be an excellent source of seasoned water for topping up—provided the water has not been collected from a tainted surface (new tiles, elderly flat roof etc.). If in doubt, test the water before use.

Installing and choosing equipment

Different types of pumps

Although the bottom line with any type of pump is that it will cycle water, there are a bewildering variety of types and makes. Regardless of make, there are three basic types widely available for pond use.

Pond fountain pumps/ foam pre-filter pumps

Most mid-range pond pumps, designed to be submersed in the water are supplied with a considerable assortment of fittings. Different fountain heads and outlet fittings, attach to a tee piece that fixes to the top of the pump, most often with flow adjustment to both outlets. Flow can be adjusted to allow the volume required and the size of fountain to suit.

Because fine fountain fittings, especially multi tiered fountains and bell jets, can be blocked or distorted by pond debris, most fountain pumps come with an optional foam pre-filter to stop

Above: A typical cage pump with pre-filter foam option.

small particles from entering the pump and thereby the fountain head. Because these pre-filters are usually quite small, they can readily clog up, reducing the flow and putting stress on the pump.

There are options, the pre-filter can be discarded (unless the pump instructions specify using a pre-filter to avoid damaging the pump)

a bigger pre-filter with a large surface area designed to avoid sucking in small particles and aquatic creatures.

These pumps are designed to run continuously. Switching them on and off and allowing to stand while still may shorten the life of the pump, but routine maintenance will be necessary to keep it working effectively. Depending on the conditions in the pond, stripping and cleaning may be necessary at weekly intervals in the spring (when the pond is at its most active) or annually in low-maintenance ponds.

Above: Pond pumps are designed to run continuously but still need maintenance to keep working effectively.

Although the pump cage may clog up, either on the outside with leaves or inside with silt, rinsing it out is fairly simple. The inside of the pump is not quite as easy to access but it is vital to clean it from time to time. Most pumps have a magnetic bodied impellor that spins inside a relatively close fitting socket. To clean, remove the front of the pump, take out the impeller, clean it with a soft brush or plastic scourer and clean inside the socket, taking care not to stress or break the impellor shaft, which can usually be removed to facilitate cleaning. If there is uneven wear on the impeller it will not work effectively, although most manufacturers will supply replacement impellers, it is not always economical to replace.

but this may necessitate using a coarse fountain head to avoid blocking. A larger pre-filter can be fitted, either a larger block of foam around the outside of the "nose" of the pump or a mechanical filter that attaches directly to the intake. Although wrapping the pump in sponge, encasing it in a fine mesh cage or immersing it in a container of stones will pre-filter the water, bear in mind that the pump will still need to be removed for periodic maintenance, so choose a method that will be practical and in scale with the pond.

Fountain pumps are usually ideal for a pond with wildlife or small fry, especially if fitted with

Cage pumps

Although often superficially similar to foam pre-filter pumps, in that they usually come with variable fountain and outlet fittings, cage pumps are more robust and are engineered to macerate any debris that is small enough to pass through the cage—therefore giving a more reliable flow rate.

Although they have the advantage of seldom blocking, their advantages are also their downsides. Any small aquatic life, from water fleas to tadpoles and small fry can be sucked into the pump. These are more suitable for a medium to large pond with more fish than wildlife that requires good, continuous flow for a filter or feature.

Maintenance needs are similar to that for a foam pre-filter pump although the impeller will be more substantial and may be based more on flat plates with vanes for the impeller head than a cylindrical bodied impeller. As these pumps are usually more expensive and durable,

Above: A modest fountain can greatly enhance a feature pond.

Above: Striking use of running water, powered by a simple pump.

cage of the pump. Very few come with fittings for fountains as they are intended to supply a rapid flow though large bore pipes, usually 1 – 1½ inches (25–38mm). There are quite a variety of these. Solid-handling pumps often come in a cage with holes that define the size of solid they can process, some have the facility to fit a remote feed so that a percentage of the water handled will be drawn from another area of the pond—useful for eliminating a stale area in the pond. Some have the capacity to draw from either the top of the cage, with smaller holes, or the base, with larger intakes. Some draw solely from the base. Many feature a very robust impeller with a sensor that will flick backwards to clear an obstruction, and some have a float switch that will cut off the pump if the water level drops—the possible varieties are virtually endless.

If one of these high-capacity pumps would

Above: Caged pump with tee piece and fountain fittings for small to large ponds/features.

replacement parts are more readily available and economical compared to the replacement price.

Solid handling and sump pumps

The "serious" pumps, these are designed to provide maximum, continuous flow that will not be interrupted by most debris. They have very powerful impellers that will macerate (chop up) any matter small enough to get through the

Above: Solid-handling hybrid pump, less suitable for small or wildlife ponds, is ideal for constant, strong flow. Does not include external fittings.

suit your pond but you have reservations about their macerating ability (they will destroy small fish and aquatic creatures), many can be fitted with a foam or Japanese matting (wiry, plastic sheet mat) pre-filter that will stop most things being drawn in. They may also become blocked—so be prepared to clean out any pre-filter if the flow drops appreciably. Unless there is a pre-filter fitted these pumps are not suitable for a wildlife or small pond.

Choosing the right size of pump

The majority of pumps are rated by their flow rate, most often in liters per hour although

Above: A sump pump, strong, continuous flow for larger ponds and features.

some are in gallons, or even liters per minute. When selecting a pump, convert all pump flows to the same values to save confusion. The following section deals solely with flow as defined by liters per hour.

Once you have decided which type of pump will suit your pond (and your pocket) the best, the next step is to decide what flow is required—much of which will depend on the size of the pond and its fittings.

The key questions to ask yourself are:

?Is there, or will there be, a filter on the pond?
As discussed, a filter is recommended for any fish or feature pond to maintain good water condition and a healthy environment for any pond life, be it plants, fish or wildlife.

To achieve adequate filtration, the water in the pond should be cycled through the filter every two hours for generic fish and wildlife ponds. Accordingly, the pump will need to process half the volume of the pond every hour—so a 2,000 liter pond will require a minimum of 1,000 liters every hour through the filter.

A Koi, or overstocked, pond will need higher filtration rates—processing the entire capacity of the pond once an hour is recommended—so a 2,000 liter pond will need 2,000 liters an hour fed to the filter.

Be sure to factor in any flow restrictions, i.e. long pipe runs, UV filters and height of the run above pond level.

Do you want a fountain?

Fountains are not necessary but they are decorative and provide aeration and water movement, both of which are beneficial to water quality. In a small pond, allow 1,000 liters for a fountain, any larger and the spray will be high enough to be blown out of the pond. Larger ponds can support larger fountains without dwarfing the pond or causing excessive water loss. For a pond 10ft x 10ft (3m x 3m) with a medium fountain head fitted, a flow of 2,500 liters would be adequate. A geyser (low level

spout) can be up to 5,000 liters without seeming too large—but it will greatly disturb the surface and disrupt floating plants. For most medium to large ponds 3,000 liters will provide an adequate fountain, depending on the fountain head chosen.

What about a waterfall or cascade?

The majority of commercially available waterfalls have a recommended water flow of 3,000–4,000 liters, which will give a good flow on a fall 1 foot (30cm) wide. A self-build, split,

Below: The multi use of a pump.

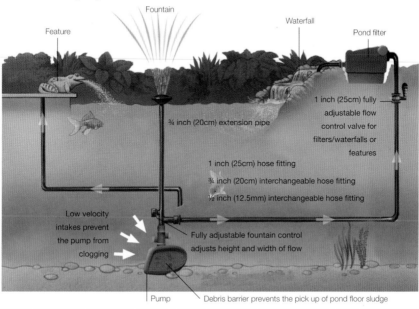

Feature

Fountain

Waterfall

Pond filter

¾ inch (20cm) extension pipe

1 inch (25cm) fully adjustable flow control valve for filters/waterfalls or features

1 inch (25cm) hose fitting

¾ inch (20cm) interchangeable hose fitting

½ inch (12.5mm) interchangeable hose fitting

Low velocity intakes prevent the pump from clogging

Fully adjustable fountain control adjusts height and width of flow

Pump

Debris barrier prevents the pick up of pond floor sludge

83

Above: At its simplest, a fountain pump turns this small pond into a feature with a geyser effect.

wider or very tall waterfall will need an estimated flow. Your local aquatic center should be able to advise the probable flow requirements if supplied with the design, size and height of the fall, although the rate of flow is a matter of personal preference. Generally it is adequate to guesstimate the achievable flow requirement at just over 3,000 liters per foot (30cm) width for a waterfall up to 3 feet (just under 1m) high. 5,000 liters for a raging torrent. If entirely unsure of the flow necessary, ask your retailer's advice and request the leeway to upgrade a pump (if returning it in resalable condition) should it prove inadequate.

Factor in any flow restrictions before deciding the flow required, i.e. long pipe runs, UV filters and height of the run above pond level.

? **Thinking about an additional feature?**
From spilling urns to elaborate spitters, spouting or spitting statues, plaques and natural-looking features, the variety of pond side features is almost endless. Defining the flow required for each one is not simple but there are some guidelines, generally defined by the internal diameter of the outlet into the feature. A very modest feature with a ½ inch (6mm) wide pipe will require 400–600 liters an hour—any more and the water will jet out, possibly missing the feature and maybe even overshooting the pond! A wider outlet can take more flow. A large, wall-mounted spout with a 1 inch (2.5cm) pipe can take a flow from 1,000 up to 3,000 liters, depending on the width of the pond beneath.

Taking a drawing or photo of the feature to an aquatic center and defining the flow on features that are sized similarly to yours may be the best way to proceed, although knowledgeable staff will be able to offer an informed estimate. If the feature is only to be operating intermittently it would be appropriate to either run it off a separate pump, or put a flow diverter in the feed hose to allow water to be diverted back into the pond if the feature is not in use.

To define the size of pump then:
Add up all the different liter totals needed by your pond and its associated features—then comes the tricky part. It is necessary to factor in the type of filter or feature, the distance from the pond, the height above the pond, the size of hose and internal filter restrictions.

Above: A simple system to divert flow from a top pond, in this case it is an annual event when the smaller pool is full of frog spawn.

Above: A similar geyser effect in a large pond is equally effective.

For example, a pressurized filter can provide considerable resistance but unless it is completely clean, 10% of the flow rate may be lost to media restriction. If the water is being fed a distance to the filter, or lifted above the level of the pond, up to 20% of the flow may be lost. If the feed is considerable (to the other end of a long stream or to a high water feature/cascade) even more flow will be sacrificed. Most

Above: Not all the flow need be visible. Here, the majority of the flow feeds through a remote filter although a small amount is directed to the vase feature.

pumps will carry information on their realizable flow at certain heights—worth considering.

If there is a UV unit fitted in the filter or as an in-line addition, the water will be further restricted and flow should be adjusted to compensate. However, be sure to check the recommended flow for the UV unit as it will be rendered ineffective if the flow is too fast.

As a rule of thumb, allowing for the fact that a pump will drop off in performance with age, work out the literage you wish to achieve, add on a percentage to allow for any restrictions on the flow, add 25% to allow for wear, then round the figure up to the nearest 500 liters. If in doubt always buy a larger pump than you need, you will seldom require it to do less than initially defined.

Other pond equipment

This is an easy area to start, but almost impossible to finish, as pond equipment is constantly being redefined, invented and changed, even if many additional pond items have the short term appeal of a gadget. However, many additions have stood the test of time and proved their usefulness.

Filters

An essential addition for a pond with fish to support the stocking levels we demand of a garden pond. On the simplest level are those that are attached almost directly to the pump, in the pond.

In-pond and pre-filters

Even the simplest of small foams set inside the nose of a pump will filter the water mechanically (remove solids) although they will have very little impact as a biological filter because of their size. The sponge will clog up periodically, washing it out will improve the water flow. Even the relatively small amount of debris removed from the pond during washing will make a contribution to the long-term condition.

One step up from a small foam inside the pump housing is a larger block of foam pushed over the outside of the inlet cage, which is much recommended for wildlife ponds as the larger surface area has lesser pressure from the pump intake and is less likely to trap small creatures. The same applies to these blocks as the in-pump blocks, they will make possible removal of some pond debris and will supply some biological filtration in the pond.

The next step up is a fitted pre-filter. There are a variety on the market that range from a 4 inch (10cm) deep disc 18 inches (45cm) in diameter, to a sealed canister, a domed, multi-chambered box and rectangular boxes. The intake of the pump is connected directly to the filter so that all incoming water is pulled through the media. These filters vary in their efficiency but most supply good mechanical filtration and a reasonable element of biological filtration, depending on the media used. These are a good solution for a pond without the external space or facility for an external filter, like self-contained patio ponds for instance. The downside with them is that they can be messy to clean.

Through the years, different companies have put combined filters, pumps and decorative lights or UV's in one in-pond unit. Although most of these do part of their job sometimes, as yet, almost all combined units are limited in their effectiveness.

A completely different solution that should not be overlooked for small fish ponds and container ponds are the wide range of filters designed and sold for fish tanks. Most consist of a removable body containing media through which the water is pulled before being discharged through an outlet, usually at the top, providing similar water movement and aeration

Above: Tucked away behind a waterfall this filter box is only obvious with the lid raised for inspection.

as a pond pump. Just one note of caution, if using a fish tank filter, make sure that it is plugged, or wired, into a GFI outlet as with any external electrical appliance.

Common external filters

Making a sweeping generalization, there are two basic types of external filters, which between them are the preferred types for the majority of garden ponds. Some contain integral UV water clarifiers which will require electricity; the filter itself will not.

Gravity filters

At its most basic, a gravity return filter is a box of media above the level of the pond. The submerged pump supplies it with water which passes through the media and flows back into the pond. Traditionally the biological media used were beads or lengths of cut, corrugated hose, both providing an enormous surface area for good bacteria to colonize. The media would be topped off with up to four layers of foam of varying density. If the foam clogged up, the water would bypass them to flow back into the pond.

There are now a bewildering variety of designs of gravity filters, with brushes to catch large debris, foam blocks, sintered glass media, ripple stacks, centrifugal chambers, impregnated carbon sheets, pre-filter meshes and UV units. It is surprising how complicated a plastic box of media can get!

All will do a similar job to different degrees,

and all have similar advantages and draw backs.

If flow is reduced by clogged up media the water will either overflow or bypass the filtration, rendering it useless. A more frequent concern is that, from an aesthetic point of view, few of these filters are very attractive but will have to be relatively close to the pond because a long or convoluted return pipe could compromise the

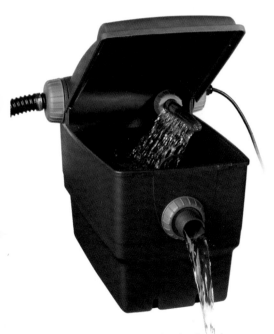

Above: An open gravity filter showing how the water passes through the sealed UV unit and then onto the media inside before returning to the pond.

return, causing overflow and water loss.

Things to check: that the filter is large enough to cope with the volume of the pond and the output from the pump, and that the flow through the UV unit is not over the recommended capacity. Make sure the outlet pipes are as big as, or bigger than, the intake pipes, and place the box level; it may overflow if it is at an angle.

Generally the filter of choice for overstocked, or koi ponds, gravity return filters are usually long lasting and reliable. The complexity of this type increases with their size. Larger models are supplied in a modular form so that the media and function can be defined to suit the individual pond.

Pressurized filters

Easily distinguished from a gravity filter, a pressurized filter is a sealed unit containing mechanical and biological filter media (and often a UV unit). As the name implies, water goes through under pressure. Therefore the filter can be remote from the pond, tucked into a corner, under a waterfall, etc., and far less intrusive. On the downside, as the water is forced through the media it spends far less time in the filter and achieves a lesser amount of biological filtration.

The water returning to the pond can be directed through a feature, into a top pond or a cascade quite discreetly. Again, there are an extraordinary variety of pressurized filters, some with a backwash facility that claims to clean the

1 Flow out to a pond or waterfall.
2 Flow in from the pond pump.
3 Cyclone flow: the filter causes fine waste to stick together improving efficiency.
4 Green water treated by UV.
5 Filter cleaning has been dramatically reduced through the use of unique triple-action high-surface area foam pads.
6 Biospheres help to create healthy water for fish through biological filtration.

Above: A cross section of a pressurized filter.

media, some with extra biological media, carbon sponges, fine and coarse sponges, even colored indicators to show clogging.

Although a pressurized filter can be more awkward to clean out than a gravity box the reason usually lies not with its design but more often in its placing, as they lend themselves to being hidden away or buried in the ground.

Things to check: will the filter be able to cope with the amount of water flow you want to realize for a cascade of feature? If not, split the feed from the pump so that a proportion of the water bypasses the filter and makes a separate supply, or get a bigger filter; it will need cleaning out less often.

Before you buy, check the cost and availability of replacement UV bulbs and canister-sealing rings. If the bulb is a branded make it may prove quite expensive or hard to source annually and if the sealing ring is lost or damaged the filter is unusable. Might be worth getting a spare?

Natural filters

In a natural body of water the filtration takes place in the planted banks and base of the pond. Reproducing this in a garden pond is most often achieved by constructing a separate pool, at least slightly above the main pond. This can be planted with filtering plants, possibly on a bed of large gravel or stones. The flow from the pump is fed into the back or base of the filter bed, preferably from below so the water rises through the planted bed before it flows back into the pond. Although a relatively low-cost option, one clear disadvantage is that, in the same way that planted areas of lakes, ponds and rivers encroach upon the water as they clog up with debris, your filter bed will eventually reach saturation, being full of roots and debris. It is a major job clearing out a natural filter, but on the plus side they can be both attractive and functional.

Above: Hiding a gravity return filter behind a built waterfall is a discreet option.

Ultraviolet filters (Clarifiers)

Hailed when they were first introduced as the one step answer to clear ponds, UV's are not always as effective as manufacturers might wish, but they are a valuable tool in controlling suspended algae and free-floating filamentous algae (blanket weed). Unfortunately they are not magic!

Either fitted as an integral part of a filter or an in-line add-on, a UV clarifier contains an ultra-violet bulb inside a clear, quartz (glass) tube. The water is treated as it passes the bulb, as long as it is not under too much pressure (going past too quickly). The unfiltered UV light damages the individual algae cells, causing them to clump together, creating particles that are large enough to be collected in the filter. The UV will only be effective against algae if it precedes the filter, otherwise the damaged algae return to the pond where they will add to levels of organic waste. When first using a UV unit, keep an eye on the ammonia and nitrite levels as the damaged algae will be breaking down in both the filter and the pond, using up water-borne oxygen.

Since the UV will damage any waterborne organic particles that pass it by, the unit should not be used in a new pond as it will greatly delay the maturation of the filter. It is also crucial to turn off the UV if treating with organic medications, or they will be sterilized as they pass through the unit.

Check the recommended flow of a UV unit before purchasing, because if the established flow is too fast, the UV will be ineffective. Also check which make and type of bulb the chosen unit takes. Ultraviolet is a very shortwave light and the bulbs are short-lived; they will only give out UV for 6–9 months. They may still cause a glow afterwards but with little or no UV. Therefore it is good practice to fit a new bulb in the spring, switch it off over winter, then replace again the next spring. If the bulb is going to be especially difficult to source, or expensive, it may be best to select a different type.

A word of warning about UV units. Direct exposure to strong UV light causes temporary blindness and occasionally permanent damage. For this very reason, all reputable UV units are fitted with safety switches that will render the unit inoperable if the casing is not sealed. If unsure if a unit or bulb is working properly do not attempt to dismantle and test it. Virtually all units come with a viewing window or a see-through section to check the lamp is operative. Replacing the bulb and checking the wiring is the only safe option for testing.

Above: A separate UV filter.

Electronic blanket weed controllers

Blanket weed (*Spirogyra*) is a fast-growing filamentous algae that thrives in clear water ponds, that are high in nutrients. It forms a strong or soft, matted growth that can resemble green cotton wool or wire wool. Not only is it unsightly but it can block and damage pond pumps and filters. Of more immediate concern is that the algae will use up all the oxygen—too much algae will result in too little oxygen, which will have an adverse effect on all aquatic life.

The growth of blanket weed is dependent on the correct form of calcium being available for it to form its cell structure. The electronic blanket weed controller destabilizes the balance of calcium in the water that makes the algae strive to grow faster. This weakens the algae and can eliminate blanket weed in some ponds.

The pond's water quality has to be reasonably balanced for an electronic controller to work, and it will not be able to make a big difference if the pond is saturated with nitrates or the pH is too high, but it can make a real contribution in a well-managed pond.

Depending on the environmental conditions in the pond, the full effects on the blanket weed might take three months to become apparent. It is not a quick fix but a long-term treatment. If it does work well, take into consideration that any treatment killing blanket weed or algae will leave decaying matter in the filter and to a lesser extent in the pond. These dead cells will use up oxygen during their decay, so make sure water movement is maintained and use a sludge-consuming treatment annually.

Above: Floating, soft blanket weed. Obscures the view of the pond and is unsightly.

Above: Stronger blanket weed underwater can be lifted out by twisting onto a stick.

Lighting

With the recent advances in light-emitting diode (LED) technology, the nature of submersible lighting is changing considerably, but the functions of lights remain constant.

Carefully placed lighting will have a huge impact on the pond at night. Light travels through water and if placed below running or spouting water the light will appear to be traveling up the moving water with great effect.

There are two main types of light, regardless of bulb construction:

Floodlights give a diffuse, wide-spread light with soft edges for low-impact light spread.

Spotlights give a focused, hard-edged beam that can be used to highlight a specific feature. More dramatic than a floodlight, it will become less

Above: Submersible spotlight with "shoe" for stability and weighting to hold in position.

focused and more diffuse underwater.

Both types are available in many forms, either pond side, with ground spikes, stands or brackets for fixing to a support or fully submersible, most often with base plates to be weighted down for stability.

Make sure lights are suitable for pond use—not all cable connections or garden lights are waterproof. Also beware of using lights stated as solely for submersible use outside the pond. They may very well overheat if designed to be water cooled and could cause a real fire hazard in vegetation.

Many pond lights have halogen bulbs, some with built-in reflectors, and many are now fitted with LEDs. The bulbs fitted will often be specific to that make, type and size of light. Ensure spare bulbs are available before purchase because lights will need the bulbs replaced from time to time. Incidentally, make sure any lights in or around the pond are accessible—you will not want to have to put on a wet suit just to

Above: Spotlights can be effective both outside the pond and underwater.

Above: Carefully placed lighting will have a huge impact on your pond.

change a bulb.

With the addition of colored filters and careful placement, a pond can be much enhanced by traditional lighting. A fountain with a lit fountain head can look striking as the fountain itself will carry the light.

More contemporary units are available with spouts of water that are lit up—often in changing, rather improbable colors—but the effect can be exciting if it suits your pond.

Above: Make sure lights are suitable for pond use – not all cable connections or garden lights are waterproof.

Solar lights are becoming more practical, and they can now incorporate light-sensitive switching so that the stored solar power is not used until it gets dark. Solar lights lend themselves to free-floating units as there are no wires to inhibit their movement on the surface.

One underestimated use of pond lighting is safety. At night, any pond in an unlit garden is an accident waiting to happen to house guests. A couple of submersed lights or a rope light to delineate the edge of the pond will make it far more visible.

Obviously, all these forms of lighting, except for the solar lights, will need electricity. Not a huge amount perhaps, but they will require dedicated power and should be either on a GFCI panel or on a time switch (again, to a GFI outlet). There is no tremendous advantage to pond lights during full daylight, and they will have nominal impact. They will need to be turned on as twilight

Above: A fountain with a lit fountain head can look striking as the fountain itself will carry the light.

Above: Switch lighting off overnight if you have fish.

falls, and off again later in the evening, as it is going to cause your fish considerable stress if the pond remains lit overnight.

There are radio-controlled and other remote systems on the market to manage lights and pond features and, although complicated and expensive, electrical works may be necessary for some lighting, there are many affordable, simple to install, and practical lighting systems available.

Frost protectors

Frost is not going to harm most pond inhabitants, but a prolonged cold spell can cause real pond problems, specifically to above-ground fittings which can, and should, be protected from frost as freezing over will likely split pipes and fittings.

What will cause considerable problems is if the pond ices over for more than a couple of hours. The supply of oxygen to the water will be

Above: Keep a small area of the pond free of ice to prevent the build up of gases from organic matter in the water.

reduced and the gases produced within the pond by decaying organic matter will not be able to dissipate. They will build up under the ice, raising the pressure and poisoning the aquatic life. It is very important that these gases can escape, and keeping one area of the pond free of ice will save the pond from "crashing."

Although there are a number of ways of keeping an area ice-free, one of the most trouble- free and reliable is a pond heater. The name is slightly misleading as the unit will not heat an entire pond, but only keep a small area clear of ice, which is enough to stave off a complete ice-over. It is strongly advisable to have a pond heater on a timer or light-sensitive switch.

Surface skimmers

A real problem in some ponds are floating debris and invasive surface floating plants (duckweed is the most common). Skimmers will suck the surface water through to a filter that will collect any particles or debris before returning the water to the pond. Skimmers are seldom necessary in modest ponds, and are most often used in large, unplanted ponds such as koi tanks.

Below: Skimmers are most often used in large, unplanted ponds such as koi tanks.

Planting

Opinions, and uses of, pond plants are a very personal choice as are the plants in the rest of a garden, in the same way that one person's preferred plants are another's weeds. No one can define which plants are the "right" ones for your pond, the right ones are the ones you choose that grow well in your pond.

Hopefully, you will have planting shelves or ledges in your pond for positioning plants, but if not, there are options. Either build up shelves with bricks or blocks (making sure they will not taint the water) or make use of large, perforated plastic trays or crates generally used for transport and storage.

There are some guidelines to help you define your choices:

Planting zones

Different plants need different conditions. With pond plants, not only is the situation (full sun/shade) pertinent, the optimum depth of water is key. There are four basic planting groups, although lilies, being such a diverse habit plant, deserve a class of their own:

Marginals

The largest and most diverse range of pond plants are the marginals, so called because they will establish on the margins of the pond. Some are "bog" plants that will grow best partially in the water, others up to 10 inches (25cm) below the surface. Once established, most of the defined planting depths can be varied to a certain extent. Thankfully, the majority of commercially available pond plants are sold with planting advice defining the suitable depths and situations for each plant.

Deep marginals

A far smaller group of plants, deep marginals may often take a season to establish properly and should not be planted any shallower than advised as they will be scorched or frost damaged in too little water.

Deep water

"Deep" is usually defined as more than 18 inches (45cm) below the surface. Although these plants may cope in shallower water during mild weather, they will need to be lowered into their preferred depth as they grow.

Lilies

Although generally considered a deep-water plant, Pygmy Lilies can cope with relatively shallow planting, a minimum of 6 inches (15cm) is recommended. Larger lilies are usually more at home in 2–3 feet (60–90cm) of water, there are few that will be able to grow in more than 4 feet (120cm). Lilies are not fans of fast-moving or splashing water and will grow away from any turbulence, they are best suited to calm areas of the pond. They require lowering into their preferred depth gradually as do other deep-water plants. All will require fertilizing at least annually, preferably in the spring or fall, otherwise they will establish slower in the spring and may not flower.

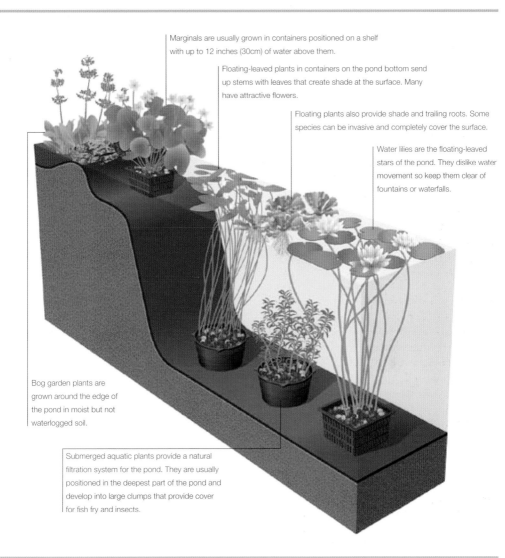

Marginals are usually grown in containers positioned on a shelf with up to 12 inches (30cm) of water above them.

Floating-leaved plants in containers on the pond bottom send up stems with leaves that create shade at the surface. Many have attractive flowers.

Floating plants also provide shade and trailing roots. Some species can be invasive and completely cover the surface.

Water lilies are the floating-leaved stars of the pond. They dislike water movement so keep them clear of fountains or waterfalls.

Bog garden plants are grown around the edge of the pond in moist but not waterlogged soil.

Submerged aquatic plants provide a natural filtration system for the pond. They are usually positioned in the deepest part of the pond and develop into large clumps that provide cover for fish fry and insects.

Floating

On the surface, clearly, is the position for floating plants. Some "floaters" will merrily colonize margins and pond edges, others will prefer to be adrift in deeper water. Few floating plants will thrive in fast-moving or turbulent water. Their floating roots provide an ideal habitat for small pond creatures.

Acquiring pond plants

Unless you know a number of people with established ponds that are offering to provide you with plants, the usual way to source them is from an aquatic or garden center. It is at the point of sale that many marginals lose out, because in order to be portable and accessible, plants are most often displayed and sold as small plants in 1 to 5 liter pots, and kept in shallow water. Clearly, in small pots and shallow water, a plant that is best suited to growing immersed in water will not thrive, so you will have to virtually take it on trust that the plant you buy will grow as advertised. The labeling on many plants and display signs can be informative, as can staff, but frequently it is seeing mature, healthy plants growing in established ponds that will illustrate them best.

Deep marginals and large-scale plants pose particular problems regarding transportation and introduction. It is fairly self-evident that a lily with fragile, 3 feet (90cm) stalks is not going to travel well.

When choosing, familiarize yourself with the plants available and be prepared to pick plants that will compliment the scale, situation and feel of your pond. Even if your source of plants is a friend, bought or given, plants will need to be properly potted while they are a manageable size. Reject any that have "munched" leaves, as it is never a good idea to introduce a destructive pest to the pond. Choose plants with strong, young growth and as many growing points in the pot as possible, as more than one growing stem indicates a healthy root system.

Be aware that the further a plant is from its original form, the less vigorous it will be. For instance, the Marsh Marigold is very vigorous and free-growing, invariably the first plant to show in the spring and provide early cover. The white- and double-flowered versions will establish later, spread less vigorously and grow to only two thirds of the height. It is prudent to make use of the hybrid versions of larger plants for small ponds.

Repotting plants

There has been a veritable explosion in the range of pond planting accessories over the past few years to satisfy the growing interest in domestic ponds.

Still widely available are the staple range of aquatic planting baskets. Although they will vary in size, shape, rim strength and color they will all have meshed sides and base in common to allow for free water flow through the basket. It used to be common practice to

PREPARE PLANTS FOR POTTING

1 Many floating-leaved plants are propagated by runners. These are easy to divide using a sharp pair of scissors to cut the runner each side of the plantlet. Make the cut as close to the crown of the plantlet as possible.

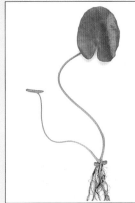

2 Select the larger plantlets for repotting and discard the smallest ones. Ideally a plantlet should have several leaves and a well-developed root system. Remove any damaged leaves.

3 When potting, partially fill a container with aquatic soil. Lower the plant into the central hole, position crown level with soil surface and backfill the hole. Topdress with aquarium gravel.

REPOTTING WATER LILIES

1 Rhizomes may be conical or horizontal. Trim off any dead or diseased areas.

2 Put roots in hole with growing tip pointing up and towards a corner.

3 Lay the rhizome level with the soil surface. Fill hole with aquatic potting mix and water.

4 Cover surface of the basket with 1 inch (2.5cm) of aquatic gravel.

5 Only the growing tip and a little of the rhizome are visible. Water and firm the gravel.

line these baskets with burlap to prevent the soil from creeping or washing out. Although burlap was better than nothing, over the first few months with a freshly potted plant the soil level would gradually drop—it was not terribly effective. There is a growing move now towards permeable potting containers that will retain soil and roots while still allowing water to circulate through the pot. Available in a couple of formats, root- (and soil) exclusive material can be purchased as pre-cut pot liners, loose squares, sewn open-topped cubes, tubes or off the roll. It depends entirely on your pond, the plant choice and the effect you wish to achieve which would be best for you.

Having selected a container to suit your plant and pond, line it as you wish to prevent the soil from falling out almost as soon as it goes into the pond, and using a good brand of aquatic soil, lay a covering ½–1 inch (12–24mm) in the base of the pot.

Do not be tempted to use garden soil, as it is frequently high in trace minerals and nitrates and is composed chiefly of organic matter that will float. Good aquatic soil has a crumbly feel to it, is high in appropriate nutrients and contains agricultural grit to give the plant some stability in the water. Heavy, clay-based soils sold for aquatic use are seldom nutrient-rich and would benefit from the addition of fertilizers and grit to make the soil more useful.

Prepare the plant for potting

Trim off any old or mature leaves and remove flower-heads. It seems callous, but flower buds will rarely survive repotting and will take nutrients from the plant attempting to flower and seed. Initially you want the plant's energy to go into establishing, not seeding.

Remove the plant from its pot, or if the roots are growing through the pot trim the pot away from the plant rather than removing the roots.

Place the plant in the new pot, spread out any roots that have curled up inside the pot then cover the rootball with more aquatic soil. Push the soil down firmly with your fingers, as it needs to be relatively compact to support the roots and exclude large quantities of air.

Although the soil will contain fertilizer, in the case of a deep-water plant or a deep marginal that will not be readily accessible after placing in the pond, add a slow-release fertilizer pellet or tablet towards the base of the pot. Tamp the soil in fairly level to within ½ inch (12mm) of the top of the pot then top off with rounded gravel (to prevent fish from digging it up immediately looking for food), or if using a root barrier membrane, lay the spare over the soil before covering with gravel.

Immerse the entire finished pot in a separate container of water (a plastic, two-handled bin is ideal) and leave it to soak until the soil is saturated and bubbles have stopped rising from the pot. Place the soaked, repotted plant in position in the pond—checking that the pot will sit securely in place. If it seems liable to tip or

Left: Even a pygmy lily can provide good cover if well fertilized and established.

fall, tie the pot back to a point outside the pond to secure it or jam it in place with rounded cobbles or other pots.

In the case of deep-water plants, don't just lower them into the deepest part of the pond, or you may never see them again. Even aquatic plants need sunlight to grow, so either stand a deep-water plant on a support (an upturned bucket, bricks etc.) or suspend it in the water so that its foliage is just able to reach the surface. As the stalks grow, usually over a couple of weeks, the container can be lowered to its final position.

Above: *Aponogetum*, an excellent plant for a medium-sized pond, has pretty, scented white flowers in spring and fall.

Introducing aquatic life

Above: A rich plant environment for fish.

Provided the water has been dechlorinated, even a brand new pond will begin to attract wildlife immediately, but it will take a minimum of seven days before it can support any creatures. Quite simply this is because there will be nothing in a new pond to provide food or shelter. If a Bio Start, or a quantity of seasoned pond water has been added then the cycle can begin immediately.

To help the pond along, add plants as soon as possible—if they have been grown in water they will contain many of the bacteria, algae and microscopic creatures that will transform a hole

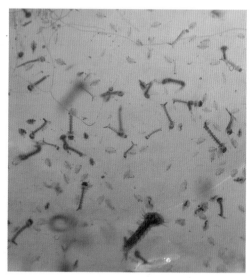

Above: Vibrant natural life in a new pond is a very good sign.

Above: Plants provide interest, shelter and stability to a vibrant pond.

filled with water into a pond. Although it is especially important to introduce plant cover to provide a natural environment and to keep direct sunlight off the water, do not over-invest in floating plants. Unless the pond is dosed with liquid aquatic fertilizer there will be no nutrients in the water to support floaters. Install, and keep running, a pump to aerate the water and if you have decided to use a filter, get it up and running—but not with any UV switched on yet. At this early stage you want to encourage some algae and bacteria, not destroy them.

Have the pond running, but unstocked, with all plants, pump and filter, for at least 7 days before considering adding any stock. During this time the filter will begin to mature as will the water. In cold weather it will take longer to establish but you can usually begin to think of it as a pond only 7–10 days after it has been finished. The UV can be switched on after 10 days but if you are thinking of adding fish, test the water first to ensure the biology of the water is suitable.

Native pond life, albeit microscopic, will have moved in by then and will be seasoning the water for you, but if tests show unsuitable levels of ammonia or nitrite it will mean that you will have to give the pond more time to settle in before introducing fish. Remember to take a pH test, because if your construction efforts have not been sealed adequately there may be an imbalance. Although there are products to combat pH imbalance, in practice it is far better for the long-term health of the pond to solve the

root cause (seal concrete for instance), even if the pond requires a partial water change to bring the pH to an acceptable level.

First fish

In a purely wildlife pond this is an easy choice— either no fish at all, or very small native fish. Sticklebacks seem the obvious choice. Unfortunately, without adequate food sources, sticklebacks will not survive. Wait until the pond is teeming with natural life, then add them. For a new fish pond, bear in mind that it is still a fairly raw environment for fish and there are many that will not thrive. Make sure the first fish you buy are hardy. Bottom feeders will have to wait until the pond is better established, nervous fish (orfe, rudd and roach) will likewise be unsuitable. Invariably goldfish or their near relatives are the best first fish.

Try not to get carried away, if there are no fish in the pond, add only a couple at first, then build up stocking levels gradually. Take care not to add more than 50% more fish at anytime because the filter will have to contain more bacteria as the population of the pond grows. Too many too soon and the fish will not thrive.

Look first for goldfish, comets or shubunkins. Avoid extremes of size—very tiny (young) fish will not always travel and adapt well and large fish will find it difficult to adapt to a raw pond (and may cause overstocking issues). Choose fish from 3–6 inches (75–150mm) and make your choices based on the condition of the fish available. If any fish look listless and inactive, pass them by, what you are looking for are the aggressively healthy fish that are most likely to adapt successfully to your pond. Since you will initially only be buying a few fish to get the pond started, make a definite choice: either decorative, highly visible fish that will have a strong impact, or native fish that may be all but invisible.

Although it is often a matter of experience to recognize healthy fish, their behavior is the giveaway. If they are active, seemingly inquisitive and difficult to catch then it is pretty certain they are healthy. Don't be tempted by the skinny fish that is in one corner on its own, as that is an indication that it is not very strong. Watch them being caught. Fish are prone to ill health if they are stressed out, and you are about to put them under considerable strain by relocating them to a new pond—it is not in their interests to be stressed to start with. Even if they are resisting capture, expect them to be caught gently.

The most usual way of transporting fish is in clear plastic bags. Take advantage of this to take a good look at your fish and before the bag is sealed up. For a start, it is likely to be the last chance you have to see them from side view (unless something goes tragically wrong). Look for a rounded belly line, a fish that gets skinnier towards its belly is underfed or unwell. Check the fins are held out from the body with the dorsal (back) fin raised, if they are clamped down and the fish is looking miserable it is not a good sign.

No retailer would knowingly sell you poor or sickly fish but it is up to you to check there are no missing scales, wounds or signs of ill health. Better to speak up now and query any markings or defects you are not sure of than to introduce a sick fish to your new pond. Don't be too concerned about the colors and marking, as goldfish and their variants, especially young ones, will change their markings and sometimes their color as they mature and according to the light conditions in their pond.

Expect the fish to be sealed in a bag with a small amount of water and over half of the bag full of air, preferably topped up from a compressor or an oxygen bottle. Make sure the

Above: Invariably goldfish are the best first fish for your pond.

INTRODUCING FISH TO THE POND

1 A modest selection of goldfish as they should be packed from an aquatic center, with more air/oxygen than water.

2 Float the bag in the pond for 15 to 20 minutes to allow the water temperatures to equalize and the fish to have a look a their new surroundings.

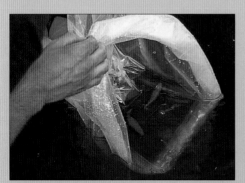

3 Open the bag and gradually introduce pond water to ease the fishes transition into their new home. Put the mouth of the bag underwater and allow the fish to swim out in their own time.

4 Just because your first fish are all basically gold fish doesn't mean they will be boring.

bag is placed inside a colored or opaque bag to transport them. Fish will be far calmer if they cannot see constantly changing surroundings. While you are there, buy a pond net for scooping debris out of the pond and some fish food. Flake or small pellets are a good choice.

When you get your fish home, don't be tempted to tip them straight into the pond in a grand gesture. Fish are really bad at coping with sudden changes, and they could go into temperature shock, which is not a good start. Float the sealed bag in the pond for 10–20 minutes to allow the temperature in their bag to adjust to the temperature of the pond.

When you are ready, cut the top off the bag and dip it slightly to add some pond water, wait a moment then do it again. Gradually increase the amount in the bag to let the fish get used to the water. Finally, immerse the bag in water and allow the fish to swim out in their own time. Say goodbye to them, they are quite likely to spend the rest of their first day exploring the pond and its hiding places.

As there will be very little, if any, natural food in the pond, feed them a small amount once a day. Remove anything they don't eat within two minutes with a net or it will contribute towards fouling the water. If fed at the same time every day the fish will soon learn to come out and wait for you, but if you can't manage to make it the same time, use a signal to alert them to feeding. Tapping a plant pot or clicking your fingers underwater for instance, it is surprising how quickly they will learn to come up for food.

Increase stocking levels gradually, adding the slim-bodied, shoaling fish and bottom feeders last. To be sure that the pond biology is developing properly, test the water every couple of weeks, or before buying more fish.

Once the pond has been established for a few months, add floating plants if desired and pond snails, they are very good at eating any dead organic matter in the pond.

Above: Goldfish markings can change as they mature.

Pond flake is the ideal starter for small fish up to 2 inches (5cm). It is easy to digest by all the fish as it spreads across the surface.

Brown bread offers an additional food source for fish. It is high in minerals and easy to digest

Fish of 2 inches (5cm) in length should be able to eat sticks or pellets which provide more nutrition.

Feeding

In a new pond, fish will need feeding regularly, but once it is established there is a clear choice to make, either continue to feed regularly or decrease feeding to encourage the fish to forage for their own food and grow at a rate the pond can support. In the wild, fish manage to find their own food; in a pond, usually higher stocked than a natural environment, they will need some supplementary feeding. Generous feeding will encourage the fish to grow and breed, which may result in the pond becoming overstocked; it will certainly necessitate more maintenance. There is no point in bemoaning that the filter is forever needing cleaning but continuing to feed heavily—the waste in the filter comes from somewhere. One handful of food = one handful of waste, it is a simple equation. If the filter needs cleaning too often either get a larger filter or cut down on feeding. It is your pond and it is up to you to adjust the feeding and stocking levels to suit the amount of maintenance you are prepared to do.

There is a huge variety of fish food available, and though most is suitable for generic fish, some types do have specific needs. Bottom feeding fish will benefit from sinking food, sturgeon and sterlets will need a dedicated food (as their metabolism is different from that of other fish) and koi, if you wish to stock them, will benefit from high protein food. The key is to vary the food, flake (occasionally), sinking food, dried food, fish pellets, live food, sticks etc. All will be well received, and many will contain color enhancers and additives to keep your fish in good condition.

Above: You can buy fish food in frozen form. Bloodworm (shown here) daphnia and black mosquito larvae. Keep in the freezer until needed, break off only what you need and defrost it in cold water before feeding it to the fish.

defrosted bloodworm

Maintaining your pond
Weekly

Try to keep on top of the debris in the pond and scoop out any fallen leaves, damaged plants, twigs etc., at least once a week. Keep an eye on the fish and take note of any unusual behavior— it will help you to identify problems in the pond. Check the filter return flow, because if it has slowed then the filter may need cleaning or the pump may be blocked up. Remove any failing or dead plants and top up the water level if it has dropped.

Spring

After the frosts are finished but before the weather gets appreciably warmer (preferably before the frog spawn arrives), evaluate the state of the pond plants. Remove or replace any that are failing, and divide up and replant any that have outgrown their positions and pots.

Remove as much debris as possible from the bottom of the pond either using a silt vacuum, a pond vacuum or a fine net, but watch your timing, as stirring up the base of the pond will lower oxygen levels. Tackle it in the morning and only remove from one section of the pond at once. If there are clearly a lot of "wrigglies" in the removed silt, leave it piled on the perimeter of the pond until the next morning to allow the majority to make it back into the pond.

Turn the pump off, take it out of the pond and give it a thorough clean, not just the outside. Take the nose off the pump, remove the front guard (it usually twists off) and ensure the

CLEANING THE FILTER

1 Look inside to see if cleaning is required.

2 Remove fine media and rinse or replace as necessary.

3 Remove any blocked sponges, trying not to let built up debris fall back into filter.

4 Rinse off sponges with pond water before replacing.

impeller body and socket are clean and not showing signs of uneven wear. Feel along the wire, checking for damage. If there are any noticeable kinks inside the wire or worn areas, either replace the pump or cut out the damaged section. Join the old (intact) cable to a new length of appropriate cable with a waterproof connector (if it is very close to or in the pond) or a weatherproof connector. Check the cables to any other pond fittings in the same way.

Run a visual check on all the hosing outside the pond. If it has frozen it is likely to have split,

and even a small seepage will, over time, reduce the level in the pond. It is very likely a tiny leak will get worse. Replace or repair any damaged hoses.

Double check that the UV unit is still switched off then take the bulb out of its housing and clean the quartz tube (the clear casing around the bulb). It is not going to be effective if it is covered in scale or algae. Take the old bulb with you to buy a replacement to be sure to select the correct one. Make sure all the seals are properly fitted when you have fitted the new

Above: Native fish are not always very visible in the pond but perch can be relied upon to keep the pond from getting overstocked and will put in an appearance at feeding time.

Above and right: These two ponds have established planting and a good environment to support aquatic life.

bulb, because the unit and the bulb could be damaged irreparably by a leak.

Rinse out the filter sponges and media (in pond water) and top up the pond if necessary, then switch the pump back on, checking that all the pipework is leak-free and water is circulating properly. Unless the filter media needed a major clean or new sponges, switch the UV back on again. Leave it off for seven days if it seems probable that the filter has been depleted of good bacteria.

If the fish are up at the surface, start feeding, but use low-protein food as the fish will not be able to digest high-protein food until the water has warmed up.

Fertilize any plants that have not been repotted, either by pushing fertilizer tablets into the pots or using a liquid aquatic fertilizer. Then step back and watch the pond come back to life.

Above: Tadpoles grow into froglets at an astonishing rate.

Above: Even sticklebacks will devour newly hatched tadpoles.

Try not to overreact if there seems to be far too much frog spawn in the pond; there is a natural cycle kicking in. Amphibians drop in and lay a lot of spawn that will raise protein levels in the pond and this provides a food source for the spring-hatching water fleas and similarly sized creatures. Awakening fish will eat some of the spawn and will feed greedily on tadpoles. The sudden rise in proteins and nutrients in the pond will frequently cause a bloom of algae and blanket weed that will subside as the tadpoles feed.

If there is genuinely too much frog spawn, contact your local wildlife agency. Most have spawn relocation programs and can find good homes for them, a far better option than a choked up pond.

Summer

Time to enjoy the pond and watch it grow. Some more maintenance may be necessary on the marginals, even if they look healthy. Rinse them occasionally with a fine spray on the hose when you are topping up to replenish water lost from evaporation. The spray will wash off any insects and pests into the water, where they will make a nice snack for the fish.

Deadhead the plants that have flowered and remove any elderly vegetation. Any visible, overblown leaves on the deep-water plants should be netted out.

Particularly in ponds with little or no water flow, be on the lookout for duckweed. It can arrive as if by magic, blown in by the wind, stuck to the feet of wild pond visitors or carried in

Above: A vibrant pond in late summer.

their droppings. If allowed to establish, duckweed is hard to eradicate, so be vigilant, and pick out any of the telltale round leaves floating in the still areas of the pond.

If you have stocked the pond with fish, keep an eye out for small fry in the early summer. The massive majority of fry will be devoured by predators in the pond, including their parents—fish do not have any parental instincts at all. Inevitably two or three of each fry batch will survive.

Fall

This is the most important season for pond maintenance as virtually all the pond plants will die back leaving decaying vegetation in the pond. Cut back all the marginals as their leaves turn brown and trim the stems to just above the top of the water. The deeper plants are not as easy to trim, so net out as much as possible from within the pond.

It is possible to overwinter the non-hardy floating plants by removing healthy specimens and overwintering them in a sunroom or indoors in natural light in a slurry of aquatic soil and water.

Fertilize the deep-water plants, either by pushing fertilizer tablets/pellets into the soil around them or dosing with liquid aquatic fertilizer.

If there are many trees around, lay a pond cover net as the trees begin to lose their leaves or you can guarantee that more of them will blow into the pond than settle anywhere else. The net

can be removed once the majority of the fall leaves have settled.

It is important to feed your fish appropriately as the weather gets colder to build up their health. A wheat germ-based food will be ideal, and avoid high-protein foods as fish cannot digest rich food as readily in cooler weather.

Drain any external features and either cover or tip them up to prevent them from holding water, as they will likely crack if wet once freezing temperatures arrive. Divert the flow from the features back into the pond to maintain the flow rate.

Check that the pump is clean and running freely, and move it to a higher level to avoid disturbing the base of the pond which will retain some residual warmth.

With the plants cut back, there will be far less cover for any fish or wildlife in the pond, leaving them more vulnerable to predators. To offer them better protection place something in the pond to provide shelter. A ceramic pipe, a large pot, or even a bucket with cut out sections for easy access.

Switch off the UV mid fall, as the water will already be cool enough to dissuade algae growth and it is likely that the bulb is already past its best and making little contribution.

During a prolonged cold spell the pond is liable to ice over. If the cover becomes complete the supply of oxygen to the water will be reduced and the gases produced within the pond by decaying organic matter will not be able to dissipate. They will build up under the ice, raising

Above: The pond in winter.
Left: It is best to keep as many fall leaves out of the pond as possible.

the pressure and poisoning the aquatic life. It is very important that these gases can escape, so keep one area of the pond free of ice to save the pond from "crashing."

An electric pond heater (on a time switch) will keep at least one area clear of ice. Adding a 1% concentration of aquarium salts will lower the temperature at which the water will freeze, as well as be a tonic to the fish.

If a strong frost does catch you unawares, don't panic—it takes many hours for the poisonous gases to build up. Melt one patch of ice, rather than breaking it, as that could cause concussive damage to the pond. Even a small hole in the ice will release the pressure and the build-up of gases. An easy way is to rest a hot saucepan filled with boiling water on the ice. The pan will be heavy enough to sink into the ice as it melts, leaving a circle of free water.

Winter

There is very little one can do with the pond over winter. As the temperature drops, most of the life in the pond will slow down dramatically. Fish will become dormant, keeping to the deeper parts of the pond to take advantage of the residual warmth in the ground. During warm spells they may come up to the surface. If they seem interested offer some low-protein food but remove any uneaten food after five minutes.

Unseen in the pond are the seeds already laid for the spring. Many of the small creatures will have laid eggs to rest in the silt, others will lie dormant until the water warms up. As long as the pond doesn't ice up completely for a prolonged period, rest assured that the pond will be back again in the spring. With proper support it will become more vibrant with every passing year.

Native creatures in and around ponds

Above: Caddis fly larva in its case.

Caddis flies
Trichoptera sp.

A family of long-winged insects whose wingspan ranges from 0.3–1.4 inches (7–35mm), of similar appearance, united by the behavior of their aquatic larvae, most of whom construct cases of pond debris for protection. It is surprising how active the larvae are despite carrying a cemented tube of shells, sand and plant matter. They move freely around the bottom of the pond and climb through plants seeking food, knowing they are safe from most predators in their protective cases.

Chasers
Libellula sp.

Often taken to be dragonflies, chasers are of similar habit. There are a variety of different species but all are identifiable by having a broader, flatter abdomen than other dragonflies. They will visit a pond to hunt and to lay their eggs underwater on plant stems. Their aquatic larvae are as predatory and vicious as those of dragonflies although flatter bodied.

Copepods

Often mistaken for water fleas, not least because they breed and feed in similar areas of the pond. Some varieties carry twin egg sacs on either side that are distinctive and make them obviously different from daphnia. They range in size from 1–3mm. Along with small insect larvae they form a very important part of the diet for small fry and other small creatures, including newtlets and predatory larvae.

Crayfish
Pacifastacus leniusculus

The American signal crayfish is not fussy about its living conditions, and can survive happily in relatively still water and thrive in waters from canals to streams and even ponds—probably resulting from eggs being inadvertently left behind by visiting wildlife. Fascinating though they may be, crayfish are not good pond companions for fish as they are vicious and predatory, and on no account should they be deliberately introduced.

Damselflies

Colorful and common, damselflies are a varied and brightly colored type of insect, slimmer and smaller than most dragonflies. Their larvae are slimmer than those of a dragonfly, the three "gills" on the end of their body distinguishing them from dragonflies.

Diving beetles

There are a number of different diving beetles, but most are hard shelled and very dark, ranging from 0.3–0.6 inches (7-14mm) long, depending on type. The Great diving beetle, (*Dytiscus marginalis*) is up to 1.4 inches (35mm) long, and their larvae, which are reminiscent of earwigs, are up to 2 inches (5cm) long. Both they and their larvae are predatory.

Above: Damselfly

Dragonflies

Dragonflies hunt other insects in flight, often over open water, and lay their eggs in water. Their larvae are predatory and grow up to 2 inches (5cm) long, depending on their type; 1.2 inches (3cm) is the size most often found. Not all the larvae develop over the summer, many types remain in the pond over winter. The larvae of the Golden-ringed dragonfly spend 4–5 years in their larval stage and are

Above: Great diving beetle

Above: The adult stage of larger species of dragonfly can last as long as five or six months.

Above: Dragonfly larva

Eels
Anguilla anguilla

A rare pond visitor, eels are rather hard to define. They are not strictly freshwater as they return to the sea when they are mature and are quite capable of traveling considerable distances overland in wet weather. They can appear in ponds, especially those close to natural water courses and canals. Left to their own devices they will move on when they are ready. Elvers, baby eels, are almost transparent and 3–4 inches (75–100mm) long when they travel upstream from the sea to mature. If rivers are in flood they may stop over in convenient ponds.

Freshwater shrimp
Gammarus pulex

Very similar to sea shrimp, freshwater shrimp are common in wildlife ponds but seldom survive in ponds with fish. They will only inhabit fresh, clean, well-oxygenated water; if they do

capable of catching prey as large as tadpoles and small fry. When mature they crawl out of the water, usually up a plant stem, at night or early morning. When the new dragonfly emerges the larvae "shell" will be left behind on the stem long after the dragonfly has dried its wings and flown away.

Above: Freshwater eels are elongated with tubelike, snake-shaped bodies.

appear in your pond it is a compliment on your water quality. They are usually seen curled into themselves, only extending to their length of 0.4 inches (11mm) when swimming fast.

Frogs
Rana temporaria

Unless you live near an area that supports marsh frogs, whatever the size and color of a frog in your pond it is most likely to be a common frog. Variations in color range from

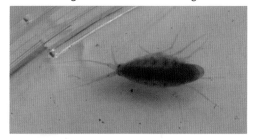

Above: Freshwater shrimp.

buff-ish yellow, through brown to greenish, few are a solid color, but they are most often a blotchy color with striped legs. Mature frogs are great travelers and may crop up most anywhere but try to return to their "home" pond to breed; this is doubtless to take advantage of a pond that has already proved itself to be a successful breeding site.

Frogs will generally avoid ponds with large fish as they will eat both spawn and any tadpoles that do manage to hatch. Frog spawn is one of the first signs of the pond resurrecting after the winter. Large, amorphous clumps of 1,500–3,000 eggs are laid in in the margins of the pond at some point during the spring—hopefully at a suitable time for the frosts to be over and pond life to begin their annual growth spurt. It is not uncommon for some to lay too early, with the spawn damaged by frost and failing to grow.

Tadpoles will mature at different rates and although most will grow up and leave the pond within two weeks, some will remain in the pond longer, doubtless as a fail-safe against predation and inhospitable weather. It is increasingly being recognized that, especially in a cool summer, some tadpoles may remain in the pond to grow far larger than usual, delaying their metamorphosis until the following spring.

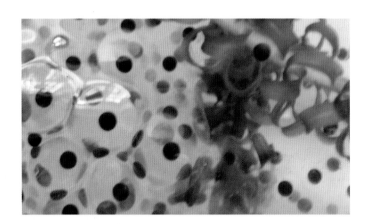

Left: Frog spawn is the first sign that the pond life has woken after winter.

Below: Most tadpoles will grow up and leave the pond within two weeks.

Above: Some frogs may take up residence in the pond if undisturbed.

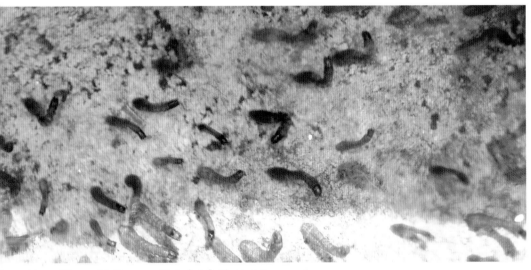

Above: "Fungus Fly" larvae settle in fast-flowing water.

Above: Hawkers are territorial and make a lot of noise as they swoop and fly.

Gnats and Midges

It is a generalization to define all the small, flying insects that lay their eggs in a pond and swarm around it as just gnats and midges, as there are many different types with different larvae. Suffice it to say that they and their larvae contribute to the food chain in any sort of pond.

Hawkers
Aeshna sp.

The Southern hawker is often mistaken for a dragonfly as is the Brown hawker. Both are found in and around ponds and rivers although they will live in boggy and woodland areas. Both are territorial and make a lot of noise as they swoop and fly. Their larvae, which are both aggressive and predatory will eat small pond life, even small tadpoles and baby fish.

Hydra
Hydra fusca
Akin to sea anemones, hydra prey on small pond creatures, stunning them with long, mobile tentacles before passing them into their center to be digested. They are sensitive to vibrations and the approach of predators and will shrink back into themselves until they look like nothing but a small blob of jelly if disturbed. Although there are different varieties the most commonly seen is the brown type which is approximately 0.4 inches (10mm) long.

Voracious feeders, healthy hydra reproduce in two ways, by growing a "bud" which rapidly develops into an independent hydra that detaches from the parent or, in the fall, by mating and laying eggs. In cold winters the adults often die off, as much from lack of live food than the temperature, but they will overwinter if the weather is mild.

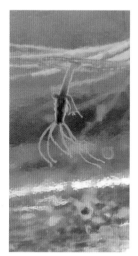
Above: Hydra

Above: Leeches live by sucking the fluids from other pond dwellers.

Leeches
The common perception is that leeches are nasty, bloodsucking creatures, which is partially true. The majority do live by sucking the fluids or blood of other pond creatures, although some will take whole small larvae, snails and small crustacean. Even if one does attach itself to you, only the truly large leeches (over 2.4 inches [60mm]) such as the Horse or Medicinal Leeches are big enough to pierce the skin. Even so it will do little or no harm to an adult. Leeches were used in the Middle Ages by doctors who believed that "bloodletting" was a cure for most ailments. Only specific leeches are dangerous to fish, the long, slim type with large suckers. Other leeches are of no threat to fish, and are quite interesting to watch, either as they stretch and compress to move along or when they swim by flattening themselves out and moving like a waving ribbon.

Above: Baby newts showing their gills.

Above: Mosquito larvae, an important part of the aquatic food chain.

Mosquitoes

The larvae of mosquitoes, of which there are many varieties, are wholly aquatic. The eggs are laid in water and develop in calm areas of the pond although they prefer still water. Rain barrels, standing and brackish water are the adults' first choice, which is hardly surprising as mosquitoes laying eggs are a prime source of food for pond skaters, water boatmen and fish. Since these larvae are an important part of the aquatic food chain they will never become a problem in a busy pond.

Newts
Taricha sp.
Notophthalmus viridescens

There are four species of newts that your pond may attract, all of which secrete some level of toxic substance when threatened. The toxin is only dangerous when ingested, however, and newts can coexist quite peacefully with fish. The Rough-skinned newt (*Taricha granulosa*) is one of the two largest of the species, along with California newt (*Taricha torosa*) and can grow to lengths exceeding 8 inches (20cm). The Red-

Above: The Rough-skinned newt can produce enough toxin to kill an adult human.

bellied newt (*Taricha rivularis*) and the Red-spotted newt (*Notophthalmus viridescens*) are somewhat smaller, at 5½–7½ inches (14–19cm) and 5 inches (13cm), respectively. Each of these four species of newts have distinct coloring, with all but the Red-spotted newt having brightly colored underbellies that they flash in warning when they are threatened.

The Red-spotted newt is a common aquarium pet, most likely due to the striking bright orange coloring it displays during its juvenile stage. Once it becomes an adult, it retains its characteristic black-ringed red-orange spots, but the skin transitions to olive green.

Generally, the life cycle of the newt has three stages: larval (hatchling), juvenile, and then adult. Typically, once reaching the juvenile stage, the newts leave the pond or stream, returning only during the breeding season.

Paper Pondshell mussels
Utterbackia sp.

These freshwater mussels are fairly long with thin, greenish shells that are transparent in young clams, and average about 2 inches (6cm) in size. You are most likely to find one when cleaning out a wildlife pond, as they generally burrow in the sludge at the bottom. The presence of mussels usually indicates good water quality, as they are very susceptible to changes in water condition.

Phantom midges
Chaoborus sp.

Although it looks like a small gnat, the Phantom midge is a non-biting midge often found around ponds and streams. In itself it is unremarkable but their aquatic larvae are unusual. Almost entirely transparent and unlike most other midge and gnat larvae, they lie horizontally in the water, leading to their name of Phantom fish as they could be mistaken for small, see-through fish.

Pond skater or Water strider
Gerris lacustris

These pond-oriented insects will arrive on your pond when it has been filled, and it need not even be well-established for them to arrive. They walk across the surface on large "feet" that are very sensitive to vibrations to detect their prey, which are usually small insects that have fallen into the water.

Snails

There are a number of varieties of pond snail which have a use in the pond as they will eat any decaying matter, be it animal or vegetable. Among the most visible are the ramshorns. The largest is the Great ramshorn which can be up to 1 inch (25mm) across. As the hardiest, thickest-shelled snails they are the most widely available commercially. The Common ramshorn is flatter and smaller at a maximum of ½ an inch (12mm). The largest is the Great pond snail, aptly named as it is up to 2 inches (45mm) long. Smaller but more attractive, with an almost clear, mottled shell is the Wandering snail, which is fairly fast-moving.

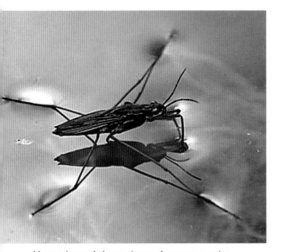

Above: A pond skater sits on the water tension.

Above: A toad camoflagued by fallen leaves.

Toads
Bufo sp.

Unlike frogs, toads do not really like water, only returning to it for spawning. They choose to live in damp places, often in nooks and crannies in and under stones, trees and logs. They are easily identifiable from frogs by their habit
of "walking" rather than hopping and their textured skin which can range from fairly smooth to very textured (usually referred to as warty). They will spawn a couple of weeks after frogs, laying their spawn in twin strands rather than in clumps, making identification easy.

Water boatmen, backswimmer, wherryman or boat-fly
Notonecta sp.

These are aquatic beetles, that can—rarely—fly, are most often in water. They spend a fair amount of time just below the surface using the water tension in a similar way to the pond skater, to detect small insects on the surface. They maintain a covering of air on their underside that makes it appear silvery. If disturbed they will swim remarkably quickly with twin paddles using a rowing motion. Only 0.6–0.7 inches (14–17mm) long, they are predatory and can take quite large prey, even small fry. Immature specimens are white or bright green.

Above: Water boatman spend a fair amount of time just below the surface using the water tension in a similar way to the pond skater.

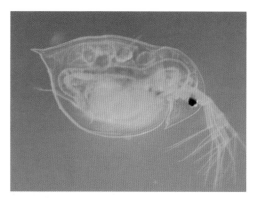

Above: Water fleas have two "arms" that they beat in order to swim.

Water fleas
Daphnia sp.

There are a number of small, free-swimming crustaceans that will occur naturally in water, the best-known bring *Daphnia*. There are a number of different types and sizes from 0.5mm–2mm. They have a transparent body and two "arms" that they beat in order to swim, are slightly pink and can be prolific enough in the spring bloom to tint the water pink. The staple diet of most *Daphnia* is free-floating algae, and as such they are the best natural solution to the spring algae bloom that occurs in most ponds. Unfortunately, fish are inclined to eat any available food and will decimate the water flea population unless there is sufficient dense plant cover to allow them the space to breed and thrive in peace.

Water measurer or Giant gnat
Hydrometra sp.

A water measurer is a surface-living insect that has a very thin, long, 0.3–0.6 inch (9–15mm) body. It moves slowly across the water and among plants to hunt its prey, and tends to avoid open water. It has fine hairs on its feet and belly that prevent it from ever getting wet.

Water louse
Asellus aquaticus

One of the more visible pond creatures, the water louse looks a lot like a woodlouse from above except that it has a dappled body, long antennae and surprisingly long legs. The female carries her eggs under her belly until they hatch, keeping them safe enough that they breed prolifically. This is of no detriment to the pond as the water louse is an excellent pond scavenger, very busy around the base of the pond and

Above: Water louse

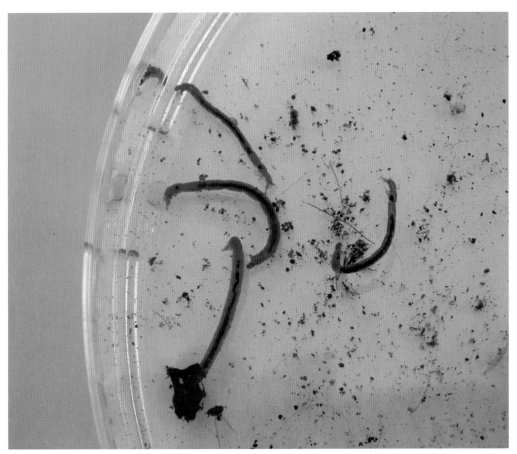

Above: Bloodworms and mosquito larvae all contribute to a healthy pond.

within the plants, picking up any edible matter. Fish find them irresistible and will eat all they can find, so the majority will be found in a fish-free part of the pond where they will thrive. They are most often noticed in large numbers inside filters, pump cages and plant pots.

Pond visitors

Bats

Obviously bats are not interested in ponds; what they are interested in are the swarms of insects that typically breed in ponds. Even a small pond will encourage the evening swarming midges and gnats that may attract these rare creatures. If you do see them regularly you should inform your local wildlife agency as some bats are a protected species. Although they have a bad reputation, don't think of blood-sucking vampires if you see bats around, they are far more interested in swarming insects than anything else. The majority of native species have large ears and look more like mice than a dangerous predator.

Cats

Unfortunately one of the most popular domestic pets is in fact a predator and can single-handedly counteract the potential contribution of a pond as a magnet for wildlife. Although few cats will take fish, most prefer not to get wet. They will hunt almost anything that moves, from frogs and newts to dragonflies and damselflies.

Dogs

The most significant impact a dog will usually have on a lined pond is to damage the sides should they fall in. It may seem silly, but it is well worth introducing a visiting or new dog to the pond and making sure it is aware of it, because if the pond is at ground level and well planted, they may not realize it is anything more than a damp area.

Above: Two ducks survey the water.

Ducks

Normally occasional visitors to medium and large ponds, ducks will occasionally take up residence in "duck-friendly" gardens. Unfortunately they will foul a pond by sifting through any silt for food. Thankfully they will seldom stay long unless undisturbed.

Foxes
Vulpes vulpes

One of the larger native mammals to adapt to urbanization, the fox is a hunter and will be attracted to a pond in the spring with hopes of catching unwary frogs on their way to breed. Although they have been known to eat a considerable number, frogs produce 1,500–3,000 eggs at once to compensate for predation, so foxes are unlikely to make a tremendous difference to the frog population. The main risk from urban foxes is danger to the pond itself. Foxes, especially fox cubs, are as playful and irreverent as puppies and will chew, pull at and damage cables, planting baskets, filters and even pond liners.

Garter snakes
Thamnophis sp.

Given a bit of peace, quiet, enough cover and hiding places to keep it safe, your pond may attract a garter snake. Shy and wary, they often go unnoticed but can sometimes be seen basking in the sun by a pond. They eat a varied diet and will confidently both swim and hunt in the pond, looking for frogs, newts, tadpoles and fish. There are more than 16 varieties of garter snake, but the Ribbon snake (*Thamnophis sauritus*) has a preference for frogs as food, and so it frequents ponds regularly. The Ribbon snake averages 16–35 inches (41–89cm) in length, and can range in coloring from black, dark brown, to tan or brown, having red, green or blue lateral stripes. Long believed to be non-venomous, it's been discovered that garter snakes do have some measure of venom in their bites, but at such a small amount that they can still be considered harmless.

Squirrels
Sciurus carolinensis

Native to mature deciduous forests but now widespread in North America, squirrels enjoy drinking from garden ponds. Their diet is mainly nuts, bulbs and seeds, but they are opportunistic feeders. Squirrels can be a pond pest by uprooting bulbs and stripping ornamental plants. Before taking any pest control action, check local regulations.

Above: Spot the baby snake entwined in the water weed as it pursues its prey.

Above: Herons are dramatic visitors to a garden pond.

Herons
Ardea cinerea

At nearly 3 feet (1m) tall herons will be the most extraordinary bird you are likely to have in your garden. Although it may not be an entirely welcome visitor it is not deliberately trying to ruin your pond, it is just following its natural instincts to hunt and taking advantage of the high stocking levels in most garden ponds. Paradoxically, occasional visits from a heron are to the pond's advantage as they will take any weak or failing fish, being the most easily caught. Healthy, (sensible) fish will quickly realize there is a predator about and will hide, for up to two weeks, after a heron strike. Usually a solitary feeder, herons will not usually alight near another heron. Herons have adapted quickly to urban hunting and will chose their time to visit gardens, waiting in surrounding trees or on an adjacent roof, until the yard is left unattended.

Kingfishers
Alcedo atthis

Although territorial and usually restricted to well- stocked rivers, ponds and lakes, kingfishers will sometimes include a garden pond in their area. Usually only seen as a flash of red and blue, this wary but attractive little bird will take small fish from the pond and will return if undisturbed.

Crows
Corvus sp. and
Pigeons
Columba livia

Although entirely different, these two large, confident, intelligent birds are not above attempting to take small fish, reptiles and snails from the pond, and it is a sure sign that one or the other has visited your pond if there are empty water snail shells lying around. They will do little harm to the ecology of the pond but they can damage a butyl liner if they pierce or tear it when grabbing for food.

Racoons
Procyon lotor

Racoons are a highly-adaptable creature with a very diverse palate, considered by some to be the world's most omnivorous animals. They can range in size from 2 to 4 feet (60–120 cm) long from nose to tip of the tail, and bear disctinctive black "mask" over their eyes. While they will eat almost anything, including your garbage, they especially enjoy fish and amphibians, and may

Above: Moorhens can be identified by their red beak.

try to take a meal from your pond.

Rats
Rattus sp.

Although true water voles are unlikely to be attracted to a garden pond, brown rats are not adverse to water and may well hunt in and around your pond. They are unlikely to do the pond itself any harm, but with their compulsion to chew, they may inadvertently damage wires and fittings. Do not encourage them or other rodents by leaving fish food on the ground.

Above: The white "chinstrap" is distinctive coloring of the Canada goose.

Canada Geese
Branta canadensis

The Canada Goose is the most widely distributed goose in North America, and is found throughout the continent. Its body is gray-brown with black legs, tail, neck and head, with a white rump band and white undertail coverts. There are six recognized sub-species including the Common Canada Goose, Lesser Canada Goose, Richardson's Canada Goose, Aleutian Canada Goose, and the Dusky Canada Goose. Canada geese are attracted to ponds in order to feed on submerged aquatic plants, by upending or by reaching down with long necks. Like ducks, they will feed on and disturb the silt on the bottom of your pond. These geese are strong swimmers, flyers and divers.

Plants

The range of plants that will grow in water is immense and includes many common garden varieties. What is perhaps most relevant when planting in a new pond is availability. Specimens can be sourced from dedicated aquatics nurseries once the pond is established. Listed here are commercially available plants and their varieties. Many do not originate from North America but have been introduced long ago. There is often justification for using non-native plants and hybrids, even in a natural pond, if they are to the correct scale and appearance.

Above: *Acorus calamus*
Opposite: This pond has a variety of vigorous plants.

Acorus calamus
Sweet-scented rush, sweet flag

A wide, long-leafed marginal plant with sword-shaped leaves, favored by dragonflies and damselflies as a support for egg laying and for their larvae to exit the water and dry. Grows strongly and is frost hardy in most situations. 3 inch (8cm) yellow flowers late spring.

Marginal plant
Height: 47 inches (120cm)
Native to India

Acorus gramineus variegeta
Dwarf rush

A non-scented version of the above but with strikingly striped white and green leaves.

Marginal plant
Height: 1 foot (30cm)
Native to Japan

Alisma plantago-aquatica
Water plantain

Quite a strong-growing plant with tall stems of small white or lilac flowers in mid summer, large, spoon shaped, well-veined leaves. Can look a little bare if planted in isolation.

Marginal plant
Height: 3 feet (1m)
Native to North America

Above: *Alisma plantago-aquatica*

Above: *Aponogetum distachyos*

Aponogeton distachyos
Water hawthorn

An excellent deep-water plant with dark green, mottled, lozenge-shaped leaves that, unlike many plants will keep its leaves over the winter to provide cover. Flowers mostly in the spring and fall but often throughout the year, with white or slightly pink flowers that somewhat resemble orchid sprays (and smell like hawthorn blossom). They are hardy enough to come up through thin ice and remain alive through subsequent frosts. Comfortable in sun or partial shade, grows very little during warmer weather.

✧✧✧

Deep water plant

Spread: Up to 47 inches (120cm)

Native to South Africa

Above: *Azolla filiculoides*

Azolla filiculoides
Fairy fern

A small-scale floating plant that will provide shade—especially useful in a new pond. Mostly yellowish green but often tinged with red. Although the fine roots provide a useful place for smaller creatures to breed, the roots tend to break off if disturbed (by fish for instance), introducing a fair amount of dead matter. Can grow over pots with bare earth, which is

attractive. Can be used very effectively to crowd out established duckweed, depriving it of nutrients, because it is not as difficult to get rid of as duckweed. It can become a nuisance and carpet the pond so thickly that it will destroy other submerged plants and make the pond appear a solid mass unless there is moving water to keep an area clear.

Floating Plant
Spread: Individual plants 1–2inches (3-5cm)
Native to North America

Butomus umbellatus
Flowering rush

A rush-like perennial whose narrow (triangular

Above: *Butomus umbellatus*

147

section) green leaves change through a dark purplish color to dark green as they grow. Parasols of pinkish flowers stand high above the water. Is rather greedy for space, will not flower if crowded in with other plants.

✧✧✧

Marginal plant	
Height: 35 inches (90cm)	
Spread: 1 foot (30cm)	
Native to Eurasia	

Calla palustris
Bog arum

Heart-shaped, large, glossy green leaves make a good backdrop for the dramatic flowering in early spring which develops into a stem of bright red berries in the fall. Grows best in semi-shade.

✧✧✧

Marginal plant	
Height: 10 inches (25cm)	
Native to North America	

2 Cut the firm stem into sections each with a dormant bud in the center.

1 *Calla palustris* can be propagated by removing the long creeping, leafless stem and dividing it.

3 Pot each stem with the bud uppermost. Spring cuttings will be plants by late summer.

Callitriche stagnalis
Water starwort

Grows well both on land and under water, good oxygenator and provides cover for the small wildlife that improves the quality of the pond. Inconspicuous, small, light green flowers in late summer. Can be too vigorous and persistent once established so try to keep it under control in one area of the pond.

Marginal plant

Spread: Depends on situation

Native to Europe

Caltha palustris
Marsh marigold or kingcup

A vigorous, free-growing plant that puts out runners into the pond (and out if there is damp soil available). Invariably the first plant to start growing early in the spring, it provides a dome of big, kidney-shaped leaves over the pond and its surround. Gives valuable cover for amphibians to approach the pond in safety and for fish coming up again during warmer days to shelter beneath until the other plants get re-established. A bit overpowering for a small pond. Grows well in full sun or partial shade. Produces single big yellow flowers on stalks similar to buttercups over a long period. Trim mid-summer to encourage fresh growth.

Marginal plant

Height: 12–20 inches (30–50cm)

Spread: 20–30 inches (50–80cm)

Native to North America

Caltha palustris alba
White marsh marigold

Very similar in habit to its big brother, the yellow flowering marsh marigold, but altogether on a smaller scale, suited to a small pond in full sun or partial shade. White and yellow flowers.

Marginal plant

Height: 8–16 inches (20–40cm)

Spread: 12–20 inches (30–50cm)

Native to North America

Caltha palustris polypetala
Double marsh marigold

The double-flowered version of the marsh marigold, many-petaled, tight yellow flowers rather like pompoms. Very similar in size and habit to the white marsh marigold.

❧❧❧

Marginal plant
Height: 8–16 inches (20–40cm)
Spread: 12–20 inches (30–50cm)
Native to North America

Carex nigra
Black sedge

A striking grass with quite a restrained habit, less inclined to "take over the world" than most grasses and not black at all. The flower spikes are black with tiny white petals.

❧❧❧

Marginal plant
Height: 4–16 inches (10–40cm)
Native to North America

Above: *Carex pendula*

Carex pendula
Pendulous sedge

An evergreen, native grass that will tolerate frost, prefers partial shade. Very hardy, vigorous and fast growing. Has a tendency to spread indiscriminately around the pond and garden, pulling out the large seed heads before they mature will help to keep it under control. An architectural plant that might dwarf a small pond but will provide excellent cover and support for wildlife both in the pond and outside it in damp or shaded soil.

❧❧❧

Marginal plant
Height: 20–70 inches (50–180cm)
Spread: Individual plant 40–47 inches (1–1.2m)
Native to Europe

Ceratophyllum demersum
Hornwort

The very best oxygenator for your pond (also good in cold or temperate fish tanks). Will not grow in a new pond as it requires mature pond water. Grows in full or partial shade and full sun. Does not root, it is a true floating plant. Seems to disappear with the approach of winter, but leaves dormant buds in the bottom of the pond, and will re-emerge in the spring. Provides perfect cover for small breeding wildlife.

Floating oxygenator
Spread: Grows strongly
Native to North America

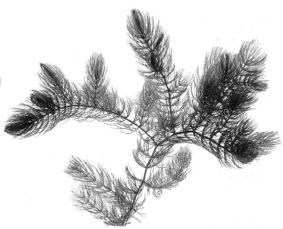

Above: *Ceratophyllum demersum* is not hardy in areas subject to frost.

Above: *Cotula coronopifolia*

Cotula coronopifolia
Golden buttons

Ideal for covering the sides of a pond and extending a mat of foliage into the water, Golden buttons has a soft foliage and strong yellow flowers that look like the inside of a daisy, but without petals, from May through to August.

Marginal plant
Height: 4 inches (10cm)
Spread: 8–12 inches (20–30cm)
Native to southern Africa

Above: *Eichornia crassipes*

Eichornia crassipes
Water hyacinth

A readily available floating plant, native to tropical areas, it is regarded as an invasive weed in Indian rivers and deltas. Provides good surface cover over the summer and is especially good at absorbing nitrates from the water, which naturally starves algae. Also provides good cover for wildlife and fish. In a hot summer it will flower, briefly, with attractive white to lilac flowers on a stem that rises 3–inches (7.5–10cm) above the plant.

Although bought specimens will be large and vibrant, the newer plants that grow as it spreads in the pond are usually smaller than the parent plant. To encourage healthy growth, plant one in aquatic soil in a pot that will hold the plant at water level. It will put out far stronger secondary plants by drawing on the nutrients in the soil.

Even a slight frost will kill the hyacinth which, perversely, is one of its advantages for pond cover as it can never become invasive. Can be overwintered in a slurry of water and aquatic soil in a greenhouse or sunroom.

❀❀❀

Floating plant
Height: 8–12 inches (20–30cm)
Spread: Individual plants 10–13 feet (3–4m)
Native to South America

Elodea canadensis
Canadian pond weed

This is the most widely available of oxygenators, possibly because it is easy to grow. Ideal for fish tanks but tends to grow very "leggy" in ponds, the older stems making no contribution. As a readily replaceable floating and deep-water plant it has a place in most new ponds and fish ponds especially as it is tolerant of widely varying conditions. A useful source of vegetable matter for fish and other aquatic creatures and valuable to newts, who find the already curved leaves an ideal place to lay their eggs.

Recommended to be trimmed to remove old growth at monthly intervals, more realistically one would recommend *Elodea* as a "set up" plant in a new pond. Once the pond is established one could remove it and go over to oxygenators such as hornwort. Can be invasive and should be disposed of carefully to prevent spread into natural waterways.

👓👓👓

Oxygenator	
Spread: Unlimited	
Native to North America	

Equisetum hyemale
Rough horsetail

Upright and dramatic plant with drinking straw-type stalks in segments with brown/black divides that grows in dense clumps like rushes. Can grow uncontrollably if planted in bog gardens or large pots. Best suited for medium to large ponds.

👓👓👓

Marginal plant	
Height: 5 feet (1.5m)	
Spread: To extent of soil	
Native to North America	

Eriophorum angustifolium
Cotton grass

Narrow, grassy leaves, fluffy white seed heads in the summer that resemble cotton wool, prefers some, or full sun. Suits small, unsheltered ponds as it is particularly hardy.

👓👓👓

Marginal plant	
Height: 16 inches (40cm)	
Native to North America	

Above: *Eriophorum angustifolium*

Gunnera manicata
Giant rhubarb

Although *Gunnera* need to keep their roots damp they are not strictly a pond plant but are included here as they are an excellent plant to provide cover, both around the pond and over the water. Established plants will grow very tall with individual leaves up to 6 feet (1.8m) across, will dwarf anything but a large pond. A strikingly architectural plant, *Gunnera* should be protected from high winds, as their large leaves and long stems can be ruined by wind damage—a sheltered position would suit them best. Leaves and stems are protected with crisp serrations that can severely scratch. They are not totally frost hardy, trim back the stems and leaves to just above the crown and insulate with straw or burlap over winter. Early in the year they produce spear-shaped green flower spikes.

✿ ✿ ✿

Marginal plant	
Height: 8 feet (240cm)	
Spread: Increases with maturity	
Native to Brazil	

Hippuris vulgaris
Mare's tail

A striking shallow or deep-water plant (up to 2 feet [60cm] deep) with soft, feathery growth on the surface, the architectural spikes that show above the water are very attractive. Remove dead or damaged stalks to prevent fouling of the water.

✿ ✿ ✿

Marginal plant	
Deep marginal	
Oxygenator	
Height: 2 feet (60cm)	
Native to North America	

Hottonia palustris
Water violet

A pretty plant that forms a dense mat under and on the water, produces pale violet flowers that rise out of the water. Good at removing nitrates from the water and providing a habitat for small pond creatures. Very suitable for small and medium-sized ponds.

✿ ✿ ✿

Marginal plant	
Oxygenator	
Height: 2.5–3 inches (7–8cm)	
Native to the United Kingdom	

Houttuynia cordata
Chameleon plant

Attractive and fast-growing plant with glossy, heart-shaped leaves. Yellowish flowers with a white surround early summer. Can get leggy, so pinch out tall stems to encourage bushy growth.

✿ ✿ ✿

Marginal plant	
Height: 6–12 inches (15–30cm)	
Spread: 1 foot (30cm)	
Native to Asia	

Houttuynia Cordata variegata
Chameleon harlequin

The more attractive and colorful brother of the *Houttuynia cordata*. Provides splashes of color with leaves that are variegated white, through yellow and red to green, offset by whitish flowers in the early summer.

✿ ✿ ✿

Marginal plant	
Height: 6–12 inches (15–30cm)	
Spread: 1 foot (30cm)	
Native to Southeast Asia	

Above: *Houttuynia cordata*

Above: *Hydrocharis morsus-ranae*

Hydrocharis morsus-ranae
Common Frogbit

This small-scale floating plant with round, floating leaves that looks like a mini lily, produces small, three-petaled white flowers with an orange center. Rather fragile and hard to establish, it will not thrive in an immature pond due to lack of waterborne nutrients. A perfect plant for water cover in a small pond. Produces secondary plants on runners to spread around available water surface. Will disappear with the first frost, overwintering as buds underwater.

✤✤✤

Floating plant
Height: 2–3 inches (5–8cm)
Spread: 6 inches (15cm)
Native to Europe

155

Above: *Iris pseudacorus*

Hydrocotyle vulgaris
Marsh pennywort

Small round leaves on individual stems provide good cover for small pond creatures, and is useful for masking pots and soil around more erect plants. Good at removing nitrates from the water and starving out algae. At home in shallow, still water, it produces small pinkish flowers in early summer.

จจจ

Marginal plant
Height: 4 inches (10cm)
Native to Florida

Iris laevigata
Japanese white iris

A small habit iris, double white flowers with purple markings May to June.

จจจ

Marginal plant
Height: 2 feet (60cm)
Spread: 1 foot (30cm)
Native to Japan

Iris laevigata variegata

Dramatic iris with leaves striped white and green, blueish purple flowers May to June.

จจจ

Marginal plant
Height: 2 feet (60cm)
Spread: 1 foot (30cm)
Native to Japan

Iris pseudacorus
Yellow iris or Yellow flag

The most vigorous of the irises. This is the natural strain of water iris and grows well even in full sun or medium water flow. Cut back the root corm in late fall or early spring to restrict its spread and encourage new growth. Has a tendency to take over a pond, will need a planting basket of its own, using a root barrier membrane or pot would help to keep it under control.

Marginal plant	
Height: 24–35 inches (60–90cm)	
Spread: 16 inches (40cm)	
Native to Europe	

Iris pseudacorus variegata

Another very vigorous iris with striped green and yellow/white leaves. Slightly less vigorous than the non-variegated form but more striking.

Marginal plant	
Height: 2 feet (60cm)	
Spread: 14 inches (35cm)	
Native to Europe	

Iris versicolor
Kermesina hybrids

A family of hybrid iris whose flowers vary from white through lilac to purple and reddish purple. Has more arching leaves than the *pseudacorus* and are less inclined to spread uncontrollably,

Above: *Iris versicolor*

good for a smaller pond.

Marginal plant	
Height: 20–24 inches (50–60cm)	
Spread: 1 foot (30cm)	
Native to North America	

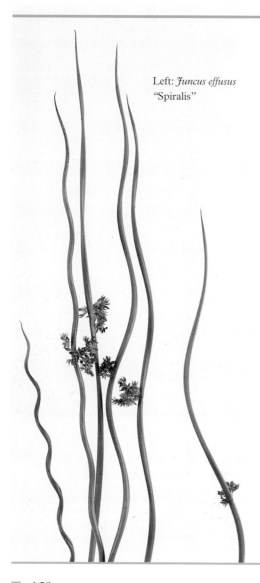

Left: *Juncus effusus* "Spiralis"

Juncus effusus "Spiralis"
Corkscrew rush

Reed with dark green, twisted, spiraling, cylindrical stems, and small tufts of flowers in summer. Provides year-round interest to ponds. Is inclined to self-seed to the (non-spiraling) *Juncus effusus*.

Marginal plant
Height: 18 inches (45cm)
Spread: 30 inches (80cm)
Native to most continents

Juncus inflexus
Hard rush

Dark green, blueish rush, very straight stems. Provides year-round interest and is a favorite of smaller damselflies.

Marginal plant
Height: 2 feet (60cm)
Spread: 1 foot (30cm)
Native to the United Kingdom

Lemna minor
Common duckweed

Round leaves approx 0.2–1.9 inches (0.6–5mm) across. The larger variety, *Spirodela polyrhiza* has much larger leaves, up to 0.39 inch (10mm). Covers the surface of a still pond in a mat that provides shade for the pond and cover for wildlife, restricting algae in the pond by preventing sunlight from reaching the water and

Above: *Lemna minor*

using up the elements that many algae grow on. Unfortunately it is very fast-growing and difficult to eradicate as it drops spores during the later part of the year that will germinate in the spring. Will clog up the pond and kill other submerged plants by cutting out the light if allowed to take over but will remain unobtrusive in fast-flowing water. Tends to arrive mysteriously, usually as spores on the feet of animals or birds.

ಱಱಱ

Floating plant

Native to most continents

Above: *Lysichitum americanus*

Lysichiton americanus
Yellow skunk cabbage

The skunk cabbage is a truly glorious plant for larger ponds. Its big, glossy, paddle-shaped green leaves are large and impressive, up to 47 inches (1.2m) long, and are preceded in the spring by the bright yellow surround of the flower spike like an arum lily that grows up to 18 inches (45cm) high. Suits full sun or partial shade. Frost hardy and vigorous but can take two years to establish.

Marginal plant	
Height: 40 inches (1m)	
Spread: 40 inches (1m)	
Native to North America	

Lysichiton camtschatcense
Giant white arum

The same habits as the *americanus* although with similarly larger white flowers.

Marginal plant	
Height: 30 inches (75cm)	
Spread: 40 inches (1m)	
Native to Northeast Asia	

Lysimachia nummularia
Creeping Jenny

A low-level, vigorous plant with strong growth that is very useful for spreading across the water, draping over the sides of the pond and covering the soil in planted pots. Despite its spreading

Above: *Lysimachia nummularia*

habit it is not invasive and will not crowd out or choke other plants. Attractive yellow flowers from May to August.

Marginal plant	
Height: 6–10 inches (15–25cm)	
Spread: 6+ inches (15+cm)	
Native to Europe	

161

Above: Mentha aquatica

Mentha aquatica
Water mint

A scented, vigorous marginal that can grow leggy—and take over any adjacent soil. Best planted in a root-proof pot and kept away from other plants. Pretty spikes of lilac/purple flowers in summer. Sends out runners that should be trimmed to prevent it from spreading.

Marginal plant	
Height: 30 inches (80cm)	
Spread: Rapid	
Native to Europe	

Menyanthes trifoliata
Buckbean

Attractive, large-scale plant with triple sets of leaves, lilac and white flowers early spring. Not suited to small ponds.

Marginal plant	
Height: 1 foot (30cm)	
Spread: 28 inches (70cm)	
Native to North America	

Left: *Menyanthes trifoliata*

Mimulus guttatus
Monkeyflower

A quite large, soft-leafed plant that produces tall masses of yellow flowers that (apparently) look like monkey faces, perhaps more like snap-dragons. Tends to self seed, proliferates around the pond (and garden).

✤ ✤ ✤

Marginal plant	
Height: 1 foot (30cm)	
Spread: 6 inches (15cm)	
Native to North America	

Mimulus ringens
Square-stemmed monkeyflower

A *Mimulus* variety with violet, trumpet shaped flowers, less inclined to spread than the *Mimulus guttatus*.

✤ ✤ ✤

Marginal plant	
Height: 16 inches (40cm)	
Spread: 6 inches (15cm)	
Native to North America	

Myosotis palustris
Water forget-me-not

A very good plant for ground and water cover, one plant will grow enough in one season to make a mat across the water 12–18 inches (30–45cm) across. The mature stems do not carry leaves and turn black, so it is important to trim it back before all the growth is too remote from its roots. Lovely little blue and white flowers in early summer.

✤ ✤ ✤

Marginal plant	
Height: 10–35cm	
Spread: 14 inches (35cm)	
Native to Eurasia	

Above: *Mystosis* or the water forget-me-not, which will create a lovely cushion of blue flowers beside the pond.

Myriophyllum aquaticum
Parrots feather

This rather ineffective oxygenator is an attractive plant that will grow out across the water like a floating mat, with the growing tips remaining above water like green flowers. It is ideally suited for floating plant baskets as it will cover the soil and spread out rapidly to form a floating island of vegetation. Even fish that tend to uproot and eat plants will usually leave *Myriophyllum* alone. Particularly useful for providing cover and support for small water-breeding creatures, it needs strong light to thrive, so it never grows too dense. There is a red-stemmed variety, *Myriophyllum brasiliensis*, that has similar habit and appearance. Not entirely hardy, should be placed deeper in the pond over winter to protect from prolonged frosts.

✥ ✥ ✥

Marginal plant

Oxygenator

Spread: 40 inches (1m)

Native to South America

Above: *Myriophyllum aquaticum*

Nuphar lutea
Brandy bottle or Yellow water lily

Native to ponds, canals, lakes and streams, this large-scale lily has large, glossy leaves and puts forth large buttercup-type flowers that mature into a seed case that looks (a bit) like an old fashioned brandy bottle. Provides excellent, hardy water cover. Is more likely than most lilies to produce taller stalks that raise some leaves above the water forming a solid dome of leaf cover. Not suitable for small or medium ponds.

❧❧❧

Deep water plant
Spread: 47–60 inches (120–150cm)
Native to Europe, Africa, Asia

Nymphaea alba
White water lily

A large, vigorous lily that can cope with full sun or partial shade. Large white flowers (10–15cm across) with orange centers, and big, flat leaves that provide dense cover. Suitable for larger ponds.

❧❧❧

Deep water plant
Spread: 60–80 inches (150–200cm)
Native to Europe

Left: *Nuphar lutea*

165 ■

Above: *Nymphaea* **Gonnere**

Nymphaea **Attraction**

A justifiably popular, strong-growing lily, produces pink flowers with white petals outside, often darkening to red inner petals with maturity. Dark green leaves often tinted with red. Suitable for medium to large ponds.

Deep water plant
Spread: 47–60 inches (120–150cm)

Nymphaea Gladstoniana

The largest of the white lilies, with big, fragrant white flowers. Grows vigorously, can establish in up to 47 inches (1.2m) depth. Suitable for very large ponds and lakes.

Deep water plant
Spread: 60–100 inches (1.5–2.5m)

Nymphaea **Gonnere**

Tight, ball-shaped, scented flowers over a long period. Vigorous and fast-growing. Suitable for large ponds.

Deep water plant
Spread: 35–47 inches (90–120cm)

Nymphaea **James Brydon**

A popular pond lily as it flowers well, large, cup-shaped double red flowers that smell of ripe apples. A bit vigorous for small ponds.

Deep water plant
Spread: 35–47 inches (90–120cm)

Right: *Nymphaea* James Brydon

Nymphaea Joey Tomocik

Lovely strong yellow flowers, usually well above the water. Long flowering period and fragrant. Large leaves, strong-growing when established.

❀ ❀ ❀

Deep water plant
Height: 60 inches (150cm)
Spread: 4–5½ feet (1.20–1.8m)

Nymphaea Laydekeri Lilacea

Lilac to white flowers produced over a long period. Suitable for medium sized ponds, not too vigorous-growing.

❀ ❀ ❀

Deep water plant
Spread: 24–35 inches (60–90cm)

Nymphaea mexicana

A potentially invasive lilly with purple or brown patterned leaves, the yellow-petaled flowers close at night.

ᴥᴥᴥ

Deep water plant	
Spread: 4 feet (1.2m)	
Native to North America	

Nymphaea Odorata Sulphurea

A robust, strong, yellow-flowering lily for larger ponds. Very fragrant, flowers into September.

ᴥᴥᴥ

Deep water plant	
Spread: 4–5 feet (1.2–1.5m)	

Nymphaea Perry's Baby Red

One of the most hardy medium to small lilies, suitable for small ponds and containers. Very deep red flowers and well-colored leaves. Can tolerate relatively shallow water (1–1.5 feet).

ᴥᴥᴥ

Medium depth	
Spread: 2–3 feet (6–9m)	

Nymphaea pygmaea alba

Miniature white-flowering lily suitable for small ponds and containers, flowers spring into

Left: Varying depths in the pond will support different types of lilies.

summer. Will thrive in shallow water but may need frost protection unless more than 6 inches (15cm) underwater.

ᴥᴥᴥ

Medium depth	
Spread: 1–1½ feet (30–45cm)	

Nymphaea pygmaea helvola

Small well-marked leaves with small star-shaped flowers over a long period. Very suitable for small ponds and features as it can thrive in shallow water but may need frost protection unless more than 6 inches (15cm) underwater.

ᴥᴥᴥ

Deep water plant	
Spread: 1–1½ feet (30–45cm)	

Nymphoides peltata Fringed lily

A vigorous, deep, marginal plant that will spread around and across the pond, giving a string of small plants linked by runners. Heart-shaped leaves notably smaller than a true lily, pretty, small, yellow flowers with a fringed edge that grow up from the water on stalks.

ᴥᴥᴥ

Deep marginal	
Deep water plant	
Height: 1–2 inches (30–50mm)	
Spread: Individual plants 1 foot (30cm)	

Oenanthe fistulosa flamingo

Japonica Flamingo

Pretty, divided leaves variegated with pink, green and white, with small white flowers in summer. Invasively vigorous. Good for cover but should be kept away from other plants

✧✧✧

Marginal plant	
Height: 8–16 inches (20–40cm)	
Native to Asia	

Orontium aquaticum

Golden Club

Slow to establish but a striking plant for a medium to large pond. Blue-green lance-shaped leaves on stalks, flowers late spring, a white poker shape with bright yellow tips. Large-rooted. Takes time to mature, do not expect it to flower in its first year.

✧✧✧

Marginal plant	
Height: 18 inches (45cm)	
Spread: 12–20 inches (30–50cm)+	
Native to North America	

Pistia stratiotes
Water lettuce

Very fleshy-leaved floating plant with extensive root systems that provide safe cover for small pond creatures, the plant keeps sunlight off the pond and absorbs nitrates. Spreads from mini plants growing off runners. Originally from the tropics, will fail with the first cold spell, best to remove before then.

✧✧✧

Floating plant	
Height: 6–8 inches (15–20cm)	
Spread: 1 foot (30cm)	
Native to tropical region of most continents	

Pontederia cordata

Left: *Orontium aquaticum*

Below: *Pistia stratiotes*

Right: *Pontederia cordata*

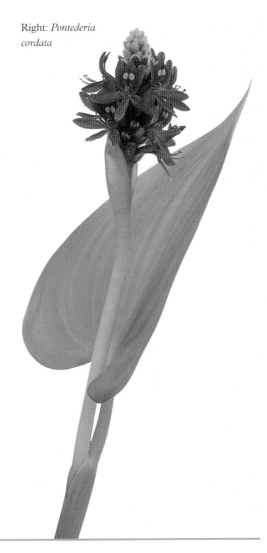

Pickerel plant

Very glossy, spear-shaped leaves with striking
blue flower spikes late August/September.
Seems to attract dragonflies. A bit big for
smaller ponds.

❧❧❧

Marginal plant
Height: 24–35 inches (60–90cm)
Spread: 2 feet (60cm)
Native to North America

Preslia cervina
Water spearmint

Although mints can tend to be invasive, this one is not. It is a "well-mannered" mint with attractive plumes of purple or white flowers in the summer. In quiet weather the scent from the leaves can be very strong—best avoided unless you like the smell of spearmint.

Marginal plant
Height: 1 foot (30cm)
Spread: 10 inches (25cm)
Native to Europe

Ranunculus aquatilis
Water crowfoot

Small plant with ivy-shaped leaves and white flowers in spring that float on the water surface. The best flowering oxygenator. Good for still or moving water.

Marginal plant
Oxygenator
Spread: 1 foot (30cm)
Native to North America

Ranunculus lingua
Greater spearwort

Large, spear-shaped, flat leaves. Buttercup-type yellow flowers on tall stalks in the spring. Benefits from free root space, may crowd out other plants. Good for a larger pond.

Above: *Ranunculus lingua*

Marginal plant
Height: 3½ feet (110cm)
Native to Europe

Sagittaria japonica
Japanese arrowhead

Attractive, arrow-shaped leaves on stalks, white and green flowers in early summer.

Marginal plant
Height: 1–2 feet (30–60cm)
Native to Asia

Right: *Sagittaria sagittifolia*

Sagittaria sagittifolia
Common arrowhead

A vigorous and attractive plant with arrow-shaped leaves on long stalks. White flowers with dark center early summer.

ఞఞఞ

Marginal plant
Height: 2 feet (60cm)
Native to Europe

Salvinia natans
Water velvet

A floating fern with hairy, fleshy leaves that will thrive in warm weather, providing dense cover and absorbing nitrates. Will fail with the first frost, best removed as the weather cools.

ఞఞఞ

Floating plant
Height: 0.4–1.2 inches (1–3cm)
Spread: Individual plants 2 inches (5cm)
Native to most continents except the Americas

Saururus cernuus
Lizard tail

One of the few marginal plants to change color in the fall, the dark green, heart-shaped leaves turn crimson before winter. Flowers in early summer with white, lizard tail-shaped, fragrant flowers.

✧✧✧

Marginal plant
Height: 3 feet (90cm)
Native to North America

Scirpus cernuus
Fiberoptic plant

A small rush with silver/white tips to the end of each leaf, very pretty for smaller ponds.

✧✧✧

Marginal plant
Height: 6 inches (15cm)
Spread: 1 foot (30cm)
Native to most continents

Scirpus tabernaemontani Zebrinus
Zebra rush

A rush with round section tall stems, horizontal white, cream and green stripes. Rather prone to wind damage, benefits from shelter or support.

✧✧✧

Marginal plant
Height: 2–3 feet (60–90cm)
Native to North America

Stratiotes aloides
Water soldier

Resembles the top of a pineapple with strong, dark green, serrated-edge leaves. During the summer it will float with up to 5 inches (120mm) of leaves sticking up from the water, in the winter they sink down to the bottom of the pond, to re-emerge in the spring bearing baby plants on stems. A very useful plant for providing shade for the pond and shelter for pond life. Bears discreet white flowers in mid-summer that mature into a large seed that overwinters in the bottom of the pond.

✧✧✧

Deep water plant
Floating plant
Height: 6 inches (15cm)
Spread: 2 feet (60cm)
Native to Eurasia

Thalia dealbata
Hardy water canna

Large showy plant with spear-shaped, olive-green leaves on tall stems. Tall spike of white to violet flowers over summer. Not frost-hardy in shallow water or exposed situation.

✧✧✧

Marginal plant
Deep marginal
Height: 6 feet (1.8m)
Native to North America

Above: *Stratiotes aloides*

Typha angustifolia
Lesser reedmace

Very long, greyish green-architectural leaves that often fold over near the top, tall flower spikes bearing distinctive, brown flower spikes, that erupt into a mass of fine white, fibrous seeds when ripe. Can overpower a small pond, keep roots under control as it can grow vigorously. As with other reedmaces, it is very suitable for natural filter beds.

❧❧❧

Marginal plant

Height: 5 feet (1.5m)

Native to North America

Typha latifolia
Greater reedmace

Broader leaves than the *angustifolia* and able to thrive in far deeper water. Definitely not suitable for small ponds.

~ ~ ~

Marginal plant	
Deep marginal	
Height: 4 feet (1.2m)	
Native to most continents	

Typha minima
Dwarf reedmace

Very hardy, smaller version of the larger reedmaces. Suitable for small ponds and features.

~ ~ ~

Marginal plant	
Height: 2 feet (60cm)	
Native to Eurasia	

Veronica beccabunga
Brook lime

A creeping, low plant with fleshy leaves and stems, small blue flowers with a white center in spring. Vigorous but not invasive, good for cover on edge of ponds and streams. Grows into fast-flowing water.

~ ~ ~

Marginal plant	
Height: 4 inches (10cm)	
Native to Eurasia	

Above: *Typha minima*

Above: *Veronica beccabunga*
Right: *Zantedeschia aethiopica*

Zantedeschia aethiopica
Arum lily

Looks striking in any pond with its large green, arrowhead-shaped leaves. White trumpet-shaped cover for the flowering spike in spring. Will thrive in partial shade. Not totally hardy, drop to 10 inches (25cm) below water as it matures to protect from frost.

🙠🙠🙠

Marginal plant
Height: 1 foot (30cm)
Spread: 18 inches (45cm)
Native to southern Africa

Fish

Above: The presence of fish brings life to a pond.

Obviously, your choice of fish will depend on the type and size of pond you have, and its levels of management. For a wildlife pond, any fish other than a small native type would prove a disaster. A small, relatively shallow pond with little or no filtration would best be stocked lightly with hardy fish that will not outgrow the pond. The choices for larger ponds become more varied. You should always remember to add fish gradually, to build up stocking levels and to consider the mature size of any fish before introducing them. Consider these attractive options, and check to see what kinds of fish are available in your area. If you want to really see your fish, choose ornamental (colored) fish.

Above: A Barbel derives its name from the fleshy barbels around its mouth.

Usual mature length:
1–3 feet (30–90cm)

Barbel
Barbus barbus
The name of this fish derives from the four large fleshy barbels around the mouth that help it identify food. Historically caught for food, the Barbel's distinctive form is found on many coats of arms. It is seldom found in larger rivers now due to pollution. Although occasionally seen on sale as a pond fish it is only suitable for very large ponds with water courses and fast-flowing water, preferably with gravel bed.
Habits:
Mostly nocturnal feeders, prefer to swim in small shoals near the bottom.
Feeding:
Bottom feeder, carnivorous, snails, crustaceans and larvae.

Bleak
Alburnus alburnus
A smaller relative of the carp, bleak are a shoaling fish that prefer slow-moving, relatively shallow water, renowned for leaping to catch

Above: The Bleak is suitable for larger ponds.

Above: Carp were reared for food in the middle ages.

gnats and flies. Suitable for larger ponds, and well colored for camouflage, it is a relatively un-decorative fish.

Habits:
Shoaling, surface and shallow water.
Feeding:
Varied diet, quick enough to catch insects.
Usual mature length:
5–8 inches (12–20cm)
Usual lifespan:
3–5 years

Crucian carp
Carassius carassius
Present throughout Europe and originally reared for food, particularly by monks; "stew ponds" were dug and tended at most monasteries. A close relative of the goldfish, it will sometimes dig up plants in the pond looking for food. Distinguishable from other carp by having no barbels by its mouth, it will become tame as it matures—if bribed with food.

Habits:
Calm and reclusive.
Feeding:
Although bottom feeding will rise to take flies and floating food.
Usual mature length:
18–26 inches (45–65cm)
Usual lifespan:
40–60 years

Fancy goldfish
"Fancy" covers all the derivatives of goldfish that have been developed into breed types. Most common are those that—due to recessive genes rather than accidental interbreeding—have fanned tails which seem not to adversely affect their swimming.

Most true "fancies" are not suitable for garden ponds as their breeding restricts their movement and digestion, and they cannot compete with the more vigorous pond fish. As long as a pond is sheltered it can be stocked with some of these hybrids—during the summer—but they will need to be moved indoors as the weather cools.

Varieties that will be suitable to spend their summers in a well-maintained pond include Pearlscales, Calicos, Lionheads and Ranchu. Some, generally those with breeding modified eyes known as Telescope, Bubble Eyes or Stargazers, are not suited to pond life, even over the summer as they have been so specifically bred they need particular care. Definitely not pond fish.

Above: Ghost koi have become very popular for ponds and lakes.

Ghost koi
Cyprinus carpio carpio

A result of mating Metallic koi with Mirror carp, Ghost koi come in a variety of colors, from white through to black with varying metallic scale patterns of predominately gold and silver. Since becoming widely available they have been spurned by koi devotees but have become very popular for ponds and lakes, and are often called Ghost carp or Ghosties. Combining the best qualities of both koi and Common carp they are agile, quick and nervy when young, preferring to shoal, but grow prodigiously and as they get bigger, become calmer and tamer. They are a vigorous and intelligent fish that can be inclined to bully and harass other fish in competition for food. A very hardy fish, Ghosts are not prone to the ailments that plague koi and should be treated as generic pond fish.

Above: A Golden rudd is an active fish.

Habits:

Will jump from the water when alarmed or threatened, but are hardy enough that they can usually flick their way back into the pond. One of the noisiest and most demanding of fish they will come to the surface and pretend they are starving—which endears them to most people.

Feeding:

Will eat almost anything, vegetation, insect, small fry, tadpoles, gudgeon etc.

Usual mature length:

2–3 feet (60–100cm)

Usual lifespan:

Unknown, having only been available since the 1980s, but being more hardy than koi are likely to live as long, if not longer.

Golden rudd
Scardinius erythrophthalmus

A fairly active and nervous fish, Golden rudd have been bred from the natural, Silver rudd, and have similar habits but are less inclined to breed uncontrollably.

Habits:

Quick, fast-swimming and nervous.

Feeding:

Prefer live food on the surface but will feed in all areas of the pond.

Usual mature length:

8–18 inches (20–45cm)

Usual lifespan:

10–12 years

Above: Goldfish comet

Goldfish comet
Carassius auratus

"Comet" is a type that can be applied to many of the goldfish derivatives. Goldfish comets are generally slimmer than the plain variety with longer tails and fins which are often graduated in color with black or white tips. They tend to be more active than their shorter-finned cousins.

Habits:
Sociable, inclined to shoal.

Feeding:
Omnivorous, will eat almost anything from plant matter and insects and virtually any dried foods. Will feed at any level of the pond.

Usual mature length:
8–20 inches (20cm–50cm)
Usual lifespan:
10–20 years

Goldfish
Carassius auratus

The most common choice for garden ponds, goldfish are hardy, adaptable and relatively easy to keep. They are so familiar that it is tempting to consider them native—which they are not, they were first introduced to North America around 150 years ago. The Chinese were the first to develop the familiar orange to bright red coloring from the brown/bronzed natural coloring although white fish can occur naturally. Owing to unregulated breeding, many fish marketed as goldfish will have white bellies, longer fins and tails, and fan tails. Left to their own devices, natural spawning and unselective breeding between brightly colored fish will invariably result in an increasing number of the young reverting to their more natural coloring. Young goldfish are black, and if they have bred true they will come into their true color within two years, sooner if it is a warm year. The color change can take weeks, sometimes with the gold coming through in patches, other times with a lighter flush that starts from the belly upwards. It may come as a surprise to find that they can change color again even when they are mature, depending on the conditions in the pond, health and age.

Habits:
Sociable, inclined to shoal.

Feeding:
Omnivorous, will eat almost anything from plant matter and insects to commercial, medium protein-level food. Will feed at any level of the pond.

Usual mature length:
12–16 inches (30–40cm)
Usual lifespan:
10–20 years

Above: Golden tench help to aerate the pond by disturbing the silt on the bottom.

Golden tench

Like Green tench, Golden tench fulfil a useful function in a medium or large pond by foraging in the silt and debris on the bottom and helping to aerate it. Although brightly colored, they are almost invisible in a pond. It is sometimes called the "Doctor fish" as it has a habit of rubbing against ill fish—although it is improbable that they do this for any altruistic reason.

Habits:
Calm, usually slow-moving, rather secretive.
Feeding:
Bottom feeding, will seldom "join in" during feeding if there are many faster, smaller fish jostling for food.
Usual mature length:
1 foot (30cm)
Usual lifespan:
16–18 years

Green tench
Tinca tinca

A bottom-living fish, green tench are most useful in an established pond as they forage in the silt and debris on the bottom, helping to aerate it. Although very beautiful from the side view, they are usually focused on calmly searching for food. Camouflaged to keep them safe from predators, they are therefore virtually invisible in a pond, which makes them one of the least visible pond fish when small. As they mature they can become tame and more confident.

Habits:
Calm, usually slow moving.
Feeding:
Bottom feeding, will seldom "join in" during feeding if there are many faster, smaller fish jostling for food.
Usual mature length:
12 20 inches (30 50cm)
Usual lifespan:
20 years

Above: Tench remain hidden in the depths of the pond where they find their food.

Above: A gudgeon is a small bottom feeder.

Gudgeon
Gobio gobio

The gudgeon is a small fish that is content in slow, or still water. Bottom feeding, it has two small barbels, is fairly discreet and is most comfortable in a small shoal. Nicely marked but not very visible in most ponds.

Habits:
Shoaling.

Feeding:
Varied.

Usual mature length:
5–8 inches (12–20cm)

Usual lifespan:
5 years

Right: Koi carp come in a tremendous array of different colors, types, scale patterns and shapes.

Koi
Nishikigoi

Although a specialist field, koi can be kept in small numbers in medium to large ponds and treated as a community fish even though they have been bred for decorative ponds. A tremendous array of different colors, types, scale patterns and shapes are recognized. Colors range from black through red, yellow, blue and orange to white with metallic hues of most colors also available. Varieties tend to have a common body shape, but have a greater variety of coloration and color patterns. Because of dedicated breeding for these patterns, koi have become far less hardy than the carp they originated from, leaving them susceptible to disease and infection. Like carp, they retain barbels on their mouths, a hint that they will bottom feed. They are greedy, voracious eaters, well known for uprooting and eating plants in their quest for food. Will snooze through very cold spells, lying on their sides at the bottom of the pond. They will become stressed if subjected to temperature fluctuations, and are therefore better suited to deeper, larger ponds.

Habits:
Become tame as they mature. Unwary of predators.

Feeding:
Varied and vigorous.

Usual mature length:
2–3 feet (60–90cm)

Usual lifespan:
30–70 years

Above: The minnow has attractive markings along its back and sides.

Minnow
Phoxinus phoxinus

The smallest member of the carp family, minnows are common in rivers, lakes and streams. Larger than one might imagine, they are attractively marked with stripes along their back and sides. Not suited for a pond with large fish in residence as they are small enough to eat, they are ideal for small ponds with good water movement.

Habits:
Feels more comfortable in a small shoal.

Feeding:
Varied.

Usual mature length:
4 inches (10cm)

Usual lifespan:
3–5 years

Mirror carp

Another type of carp derived from the Common carp and of similar habits. A calm, bottom-feeding fish that will spend more time nearer the surface as it matures, it will quickly learn to accept food and can become quite tame. Distinctive, large scales along the back and sides resemble mirrors, and the placement and scale size varies one to another and are as distinctive as finger prints. A good fish for a medium to large pond.

Habits:
Bottom feeding until medium-sized. Placid, prefers the company of fish of a similar size and habit.

Feeding:
Varied.

Usual mature length:
4 feet (1.2m)

Usual lifespan:
Up to 60 years

Orfe
Idus idus
The natural coloring for orfe is dark grey with a silvery belly; Golden and Blue orfe have been selectively bred for their color. Native to fast rivers they will, by instinct, attempt to climb fast-flowing waterfalls. Rather nervous, they need to be part of a shoal to feel safe. They will accept rudd as part of their shoal, and it is recommended to have a minimum of three, preferably five to form a shoaling group. Although attractive, these slim fish are not

Above: Orfe are natives of fast rivers.

suitable for all ponds, as they require very well-oxygenated, moving water. Oxygen shortages caused by stormy weather at night can be enough to kill or cause spine damage, giving rise to otherwise healthy-looking fish with pronounced kinks in their length. As they can be sensitive to some fish treatments, check any medications/chemicals are suitable for their type before use.

Habits:
Fast-moving and nervous. Inclined to swim into fast-flowing water.

Feeding:
Surface-feeding, will jump for insects.

Usual mature length:
2 feet (60cm) can reach 3 feet (90cm)

Usual lifespan:
17 years

Perch
Perca fluviatilis

Native to streams, rivers, lakes and ponds the perch is possibly one of the most attractive native fish. Its greenish body has well-pronounced, vertical dark stripes, with two distinct dorsal fins, the front one very high and spiny, deep body, strong stripes, red fins and a large mouth; it is easy to identify when mature. A wary and fast-moving fish it is more likely to be seen darting from one lurking place to another but having found a place to rest, often under foliage, it will remain almost motionless for hours. As predatory as a pike; having a perch

is almost a guarantee that your pond will not become overrun with frogs, newts or home-bred fish, because it will eat them.

Habits:
Tendency to lurk in the shadows.

Feeding:
Carnivorous and voracious feeder.

Usual mature length:
10 inches (25cm)

Pike
Esox lucius

Widespread in lakes and ponds, the pike is undeniably a beautiful fish, but is inclined to be solitary in a pond—usually because it has eaten all the other fish. Its large jaws, teeth and a voracious appetite ensure that large fish, ducklings, amphibians and even small mammals are not safe from them. They are most often introduced to ponds and lakes by accident, and if you do identify a pike in your pond bear in mind that it may soon be the only fish you have.

Habits:
Lurks in still, often shallow areas of water.

Feeding:
Carnivorous.

Usual mature length:
Up to 4 feet (1.2m)

Usual lifespan:
Over 30 years

Above: Roach

Roach
Rutilus rutilus

Often confused with the Common rudd, roach have similar habits but are generally slimmer. Sharing the red eyes but having distinctive, bright red fins, their dorsal fin is further forward. Not really suitable for small ponds, it prefers to shoal with like fish such as rudd and orfe, and are inclined to breed prodigiously.

Habits:
Shoaling, at home in still, or slow or fast-moving water.
Feeding:
Varied.
Usual mature length:
8–14 inches (20–35cm)
Usual lifespan:
12–16 years

Above: Rudd

Above: Sarasa comet

Rudd
Scardinius erythrophthalmus

The Common (silver) and Golden rudd are a sociable, active fish with distinctive red eyes, of similar habits and temperaments as orfe but possibly too active for anything but a large pond. The Silver rudd especially is renowned for breeding indiscriminately with other shoaling fish and since its fry do not hatch until they are already 0.4–0.5 inches (10–12mm) long, their survival rate is high, resulting in rapidly increasing numbers. One should avoid rudd in anything but a large pond.

Habits:
Shoaling, breed prodigiously. Can be sensitive to some fish treatments, check any medications/chemicals are suitable for their type before use.

Feeding:
Varied.

Usual mature length:
8–14 inches (20–35cm)

Sarasa comet

Originally from Japan, and now bred widely, Sarasa's markings will vary considerably, although as a general rule the belly will be whiter, the back most strongly colored. Curious markings sometimes crop up, with crimson to orange markings that can range from one small dot on the head to an all-over piebald. In the same way that goldfish may change color, their markings may change depending on pond conditions. An attractive and popular pond fish, and a variation of the goldfish comet, it is generally slim, fast-swimming and active.

Habits:
Sociable, inclined to shoal.

Feeding:
Omnivorous, will eat almost anything from plant matter and insects to commercial, medium protein-level food. Will feed at any level of the pond.

Usual mature length:
8–16 inches (20cm–40cm)

Usual lifespan: 10–20 years

Above: Consider the mature size of any fish before introducing them.

Above and below: Shubunkin vary in color—blue, orange, gold, white and black may be predominant with varying patches.

Shubunkin
Carassius auratus

Yet another fish derived from goldfish, shubunkin have similar behavior and habits to goldfish, although they seldom grow as large or live as long. Their colors and markings vary depending on their breeding source, with blue, orange, gold, white and black being the predominant color with varying patches, many have longer tails similar to comets, black streaks in the fins and tails are common.

Habits:
Sociable, inclined to shoal.

Feeding: Omnivorous, will eat almost anything from plant matter and insects to commercial, medium protein-level food. Will feed at any level of the pond.

Usual mature length:
8–12 inches (20–30cm)

Usual lifespan:
8–12 years

Above: Sterlet

Sterlet
Acipenser ruthenus

Although fabulous fish, sterlet are native to very fast-flowing rivers and are not at home in a medium-sized pond. Their ridges and pointed fins can easily get entangled and trapped in blanket weed and plants, making them more suited to large, unplanted ponds. Although delightful additions to a pond due to their character and curious behavior—they tend to swim around vertically with their noses sticking out of the water to trawl the surface for food—their constitution is unlike that of other fish and they will require dedicated foods. They are not a fish to purchase on a whim. Although similar-looking to a sturgeon, sterlet are more grey than brown with white edges on their nose and fins.

Habits:

Solitary, most active at night. If injured, trapped or stressed they have a tendency to panic, which upsets their balance. If they cannot right themselves they may go into a "stress spiral" and literally stress themselves to death over a period of hours. As they are sensitive to some treatments, check product details before dosing the pond.

Feeding:

Carnivorous, owing to their liver being different from other fish. They will require a specifically formulated, sinking food to thrive, but will eat any live food on the bottom or sides of the pond.

Usual mature length:

4 feet (1.25m)

Usual lifespan:

25 years

Stickleback
Gasterosteus aculeatus

This is perhaps the only fish suitable for a wildlife pond, although even they will greatly affect the survival rates of many other creatures. Newts, for instance, will frequently avoid ponds containing sticklebacks as they are likely to eat most newtlets. The stickleback is native to ponds, streams and still waters. Although there are four varieties, the three-spined is the variety most often seen. Although not a shoaling fish, the stickleback is gregarious and active. It builds nests for its eggs and guards them fiercely, and therefore breeds successfully. A single pair can soon populate a pond. With a tendency to lurk, it is not always visible in the pond, even when tinged red during the breeding season. It does not make a good fish for larger ponds for one very good reason. The spines in front of its dorsal fin are there for protection. When alarmed or threatened, the spines are raised, as many predatory fish will have found to their cost. Stickleback will be the last (attempted) meal of many fish that will be found later with a small tail still sticking out of their mouths. So

Above: Stickleback

be nice to sticklebacks—either keep them as the only fish in a wildlife pond or not at all!

Habits:
Tend to lurk and dart. Have well-documented breeding habits that include aggressive displays and nest building.

Feeding:
Varied.

Usual mature length:
2–3 inches (5–8cm)

Usual lifespan:
4 years

Sturgeon
Acipenser baerii

Sturgeon are native to very fast-flowing rivers and are not at home in anything but a large, well-filtered and fast-moving pond. Their behavior is similar to sterlets, as they also tend to swim around vertically with their noses sticking out of the water trawling the surface for food. They will also require dedicated foods. Not a fish to purchase on a whim, especially since it grows huge, it is so unsuitable for ponds that retailers have to hold a licence to stock it and it seems registration for owners may become mandatory in the future.

Above: Sturgeon need a large, well-filtered and fast-moving pond or they will not survive.

Habits:

Solitary, have a tendency to panic, which upsets their balance, if they cannot right themselves they may go into a "stress spiral" and literally stress themselves to death over a period of hours. Sensitive to some fish treatments, check product details before dosing the pond.

Feeding:

Carnivorous. Owing to their liver being different from other fish, they will require a specifically formulated sinking food to thrive. Will eat any live food on the bottom or sides of the pond.

Usual mature length:

6½ feet (2m)

Usual lifespan:

25 years, in the wild have been recorded considerably older.

Yellow comet

A variation of goldfish, sometime called Lemon comets. Sociable, outgoing and very visible in the pond, they make an excellent pond fish. Will interbreed with other goldfish types and are unlikely to breed true—their young will most often revert to their ancestral type of golden bronze. Sometimes available with black or white markings on the top of the body, tail or fins.

Habits:

Sociable, inclined to shoal.

Feeding:

Omnivorous, will eat almost anything from plant matter and insects to commercial, medium protein-level food. Will feed at any level of the pond.

Usual mature length:

8–10 inches (20–25cm)

Usual lifespan:

10–20 years

Right: Yellow comet

Index

Useful information

The following formulas will provide working approximations of surface area/capacity.

Pond surface area:

Use to define stocking levels.
For a circular pond, radius^2 (in feet), multiplied by 3.14 = square feet of water surface.
Other shapes, average length (in feet) multiplied by average width (in feet) = square feet of water surface.

Recommended stocking levels:

For an unfiltered pond: 1 inch (25mm) of fish per square foot of water surface.
For a new, filtered pond: 1 inch (25mm) of fish per square foot of water surface, increasing as it matures.
For an established filtered pond (over 60 days with fish, filter fitted and running):
2 inches (50mm) of fish per square foot of water surface.

Pond volume:

The amount of water in the pond—needed to define required filtration and dosages for pond treatments and medications.
For a circular pond, surface area (in square feet) multiplied by the depth (in feet) multiplied by 6.25 = gallons.
Other shapes, surface area (in square feet) multiplied by the average depth (in feet), multiplied by 6.25 = gallons.

Water weight:

One gallon of water weighs 8.34 lbs.
One liter of water weighs 1kg.

Conversions:

Feet (ft) to meters? Multiply by 0.3048
Meters (m) into feet? Multiply by 3.2808
Gallons to liters? Multiply by 4.55
Liters to gallons? Multiply by 0.22

THANKS TO:

Daniel DuGard for manuscript editing and creative input. Particular thanks to Hertfordshire Fisheries, Paul Hallows, Carolyn and Ric Duffill for allowing me to take and use photos of their gardens and ponds.

31901051193920